ALSO BY JOE SACCO

Palestine

Safe Area Goražde: The War in Eastern Bosnia 1992–95

Notes from a Defeatist

The Fixer: A Story from Sarajevo

War's End: Profiles from Bosnia 1995–96

But I Like It

Footnotes in Gaza

JOURNALISM

JOURNALISM

JOE SACCO

METROPOLITAN BOOKS   HENRY HOLT AND COMPANY   NEW YORK

Metropolitan Books
Henry Holt and Company, LLC
Publishers since 1866
175 Fifth Avenue
New York, New York 10010
www.henryholt.com

Metropolitan Books® and [m]® are registered trademarks of
Henry Holt and Company, LLC.

Library of Congress Cataloging-in-Publication Data

Sacco, Joe.
 Journalism / Joe Sacco. — 1st U.S. ed.
     p. cm.
 "This volume collects most all the shorter reporting pieces I have done over the years for
magazines, newspapers, and book anthologies. As such, it seems to call for some sort of
introductory fusillade to rout all those who would naysay the legitimacy of comics as an
effective means of journalism"— P.
 ISBN 978-0-8050-9793-1
 1. Military history, Modern—20th century—Comic books, strips, etc. 2. Military history,
Modern—21st century—Comic books, strips, etc. 3. War—Comic books, strips, etc.
4. Society and war—Comic books, strips, etc. I. Title.
 D431.S23 2012
 355.0209—dc23   2011052079

Henry Holt books are available for special promotions and premiums.
For details contact: Director, Special Markets.

Originally published in hardcover in 2012 by Metropolitan Books

First paperback edition 2013

Designed by Kelly S. Too

Printed in China
10 9 8 7 6 5 4 3

To Paul Copley and Hal Swafford,
teachers and friends

CONTENTS

Preface: A Manifesto Anyone?   xi

THE HAGUE   1
  The War Crimes Trials   2

THE PALESTINIAN TERRITORIES   9
  Hebron: A Look Inside   10
  Gaza Portfolio   14
  The Underground War in Gaza   22

THE CAUCASUS   27
  Chechen War, Chechen Women   29
  What Refugees?   70

IRAQ   73
  Complacency Kills   74
  Down! Up!   82
  Trauma on Loan   98

MIGRATION   107
  The Unwanted   109

INDIA   159
  Kushinagar   160

Acknowledgments   191

PREFACE
A MANIFESTO, ANYONE?

This volume collects most all the shorter reporting pieces I have done over the years for magazines, newspapers, and book anthologies. As such, it seems to call for some sort of introductory fusillade to rout all those who would naysay the legitimacy of comics as an effective means of journalism.

But before we commence firing, perhaps we should hear out the dissenters. After all, their objections may have merit. How should we respond, for example, when they question the notion that drawings can aspire to objective truth? Isn't that—objective truth—what journalism is all about? Aren't drawings by their very nature subjective?

The answer to this last question is yes. There will always exist, when presenting journalism in the comics form, a tension between those things that can be verified, like a quote caught on tape, and those things that defy verification, such as a drawing purporting to represent a specific episode. Drawings are interpretive even when they are slavish renditions of photographs, which are generally perceived to capture a real moment literally. But there is nothing *literal* about a drawing. A cartoonist assembles elements deliberately and places them with intent on a page. There is none of the photographer's luck at snapping a picture at precisely the right moment. A cartoonist "snaps" his drawing at any moment he or she chooses. It is this choosing that makes cartooning an inherently subjective medium.

This does not let the cartoonist who aspires to journalism off the hook. The journalist's standard obligations—to report accurately, to get quotes right, and to check claims—still pertain. But a comics journalist has obligations that go deeper than that. A writer can breezily describe a convoy of UN vehicles as "a convoy of UN vehicles" and move on to the rest of the story. A comics journalist must *draw* a convoy of vehicles, and that raises a lot of questions. So, what do these vehicles look like? What do the uniforms of the UN personnel look like? What does the road look like? And what about the surrounding hills?

Fortunately, there is no stylebook to tell the comics journalist how far he or she must go to get such details right. The cartoonist draws with the essential truth in mind, not the literal truth, and that allows for a wide variety of interpretations to accommodate a wide variety of drawing styles. No two cartoonists are going to draw a UN truck exactly the same way even if working from the same reference material.

Here I can only lay out my own standards as far as pictorial veracity is concerned. I try to draw people and objects as accurately as possible whenever possible. To my mind, anything that *can* be drawn accurately *should* be drawn accurately—by which I mean a drawn thing must be easily recognizable as the real thing it is meant to represent. However, there are drawings—particularly in scenes that take place in the past that I did not see myself—for which I must necessarily use my imagination, or, rather, my *informed* imagination. By this I mean that whatever I draw must have grounding in the specifics of the time, place, and situation I am trying to re-create. In film terms, a cartoonist is a set designer, a costume designer, and a casting director, and to successfully carry out those roles probably requires research in books, archives, and on the Internet. When relying on eyewitness testimony, I ask pertinent *visual* questions: How many people were there? Where was the barbed wire? Were the people sitting or standing? At the minimum I want to orient readers to a particular moment, but my goal is to satisfy an eyewitness that my drawn depiction essentially represents his or her experience.

But, as I have implied, this can hardly be a perfect undertaking. Ultimately, a drawing reflects the vision of the individual cartoonist.

I do not think this exiles a drawn report from the realm of journalism. I think it is possible to strive for accuracy within a drawn work's subjective framework. In other words, facts (a truck carrying prisoners came down the road) and subjectivity (how that scene is drawn) are not mutually exclusive. I, for one, embrace the implications of subjective reporting and prefer to highlight them. Since it is difficult (though not impossible) to draw myself out of a story, I usually don't try. The effect, journalistically speaking, is liberating. Since I am a "character" in my own work, I give myself journalistic permission to show my interactions with those I meet. Much can be learned about people from these personal exchanges, which most mainstream newspaper reporters, alas, excise from their articles. (The stories journalists tell around a dinner table, which generally involve similar interactions, are often more interesting and revealing than what gets into their copy.) Despite the impression they might try to give, journalists are not flies on the wall that are neither seen nor heard. In the field, when reporting, a journalist's presence is almost always felt. Young men shake their guns in the air when a camera crew starts filming, and they police each other when a reporter starts asking probing questions. By admitting that I am present at the scene, I mean to signal to the reader that journalism is a process with seams and imperfections practiced by a human being—it is not a cold science carried out behind Plexiglas by a robot.

This brings us to American journalism's Holy of Holies, "objectivity." To be clear, I have no trouble with the word itself, if it simply means approaching a story without any preconceived ideas at all. The problem is I don't think most journalists approach a story that has any importance in that way. I certainly can't. An American journalist arriving on the tarmac in Afghanistan does not immediately drop her American views to become a blank slate on which her new, sharp-eyed observations can now be impressed. Does she suddenly stop thinking of the American soldiers she is following as basically decent, well-meaning countrymen who share many of her values in order to assess them as instruments of a nation-state operating in its own interest as—objectively speaking—they are? At the very best, she tries to report on their actions and behavior honestly whatever her own sympathies. As the legendary American journalist Edward R. Murrow said, "Everyone is a prisoner of his own experiences. No one can eliminate prejudices—just recognize them."

Another trap promoted in American journalism schools is the slavish adherence to "balance." But if one side says one thing and the other side says another, does the truth necessarily reside "somewhere in the middle"? A journalist who says, "Well, I pissed off both sides—I must be doing something right," is probably fooling himself and, worse, he may be fooling the reader. Balance should not be a smokescreen for laziness. If there are two or more versions of events, a journalist needs to explore and consider each claim, but ultimately the journalist must get to the bottom of a contested account independently of those making their claims. As much as journalism is about "what they said they saw," it is about "what I saw for myself." The journalist must strive to find out what is going on and tell it, not neuter the truth in the name of equal time.

I've picked the stories I wanted to tell, and by those selections my own sympathies should be clear. I chiefly concern myself with those who seldom get a hearing, and I don't feel it is incumbent on me to balance their voices with the well-crafted apologetics of the powerful. The powerful are generally excellently served by the mainstream media or propaganda organs. The powerful should be quoted, yes, but to measure their pronouncements against the truth, not to obscure it. If I believe power brings out the worst in people, I've observed that those on the short end of the stick don't always acquit themselves well either, and I've endeavored to report that. I think the great British journalist Robert Fisk gets the equation about right: "I always say that reporters should be neutral and unbiased on the side of those who suffer."

In short, the blessing of an inherently interpretive medium like comics is that it hasn't allowed me to lock myself within the confines of traditional journalism. By making it difficult to draw myself out of a scene, it hasn't permitted me to make a virtue of dispassion. For good or for ill, the comics medium is adamant, and it has forced me to make choices. In my view, that is part of its message.

JOE SACCO
April 2011

JOURNALISM

THE HAGUE

ALL RISE!

And we all rise in Courtroom One at the International Criminal Tribunal for the former Yugoslavia in The Hague, the Netherlands, for the solemn moment and majesty of...

the WAR CRIMES TRIALS

This is History, baby, with a capital H, the first international war crimes trials since the Nuremberg court put the likes of Goering and Hess in the dock...

Written and drawn by JOE SACCO © 1998; Color by RHEA PATTON

But the judges striding in today haven't brought the victor's mighty gavel to crack down on a vanquished foe...

They've come with a United Nations mandate to sort through the crimes and atrocities committed by all sides in the recent Balkan wars.

The only other time I've been to court was to watch a friend argue down a traffic fine. But the accused at today's pretrial motions, Dr. Milan Kovacevic, a Bosnian Serb hospital director, is in considerably hotter water...

Genocide: Acts committed with the intent to destroy, in whole or in part, a national, ethnic, or religious group...

The prosecution says Kovacevic played a key role in setting up notorious camps—"transit centers," he once called them—as Serbs expelled Muslims and Croats from the Prijedor area at the beginning of the Bosnian War...

Dr. Kovacevic is charged with genocide.

Genocide?

Him?

J. SACCO 6.98

2

The tribunal has already heard what went on in those camps at the trial of Dusko Tadic, a Bosnian Serb and former karate instructor...

Witness after witness described the living conditions...

the interrogations, the killings...

and the cases of sexual assault...

Q: "WERE YOU ORDERED TO LICK HIS ARSE, MR. H?"

"YES"

Q: "WAS MR. G ORDERED TO SUCK HIS PENIS?"

"YES"

Q: "WAS THE NEXT ORDER FOR MR. G TO BITE HIS TESTICLES?"

"YES"

BITE! HARDER! HARDER!

And Mr. G bit off the man's testicle.

The victim, Fikret Harambasic, wasn't the only Muslim savaged that day. Witnesses saw bloody bodies, a man being cut as "one slices chops," but the court said no deaths had been proven. It noted, though, that four of those assaulted, including Harambasic, were never seen again.

After the war, before he was nabbed by British soldiers, Dr. Kovacevic told a reporter—

WHAT WE DID WAS THE SAME AS AUSCHWITZ OR DACHAU, BUT IT WAS A MISTAKE.

IT WAS PLANNED TO HAVE BEEN A CAMP, BUT NOT A CONCENTRATION CAMP.

One of his attorneys, Anthony D'Amato, a professor at Northwestern Law School, tells me that Kovacevic wanted to resign from the council overseeing the operation, but—

THEY SAID THEY WOULD SHOOT HIM.

HE HAD HEARD ABOUT THE ATROCITIES IN THE CAMPS.

HE DIDN'T WANT TO BE PART OF THE SCENE ANYMORE.

J. SACCO 6-98

The scene, the scene...

That and other scenes were played out years ago and hundreds of miles away...

I was in Bosnia in the fall and early winter of '95–'96...

One scene after another was re-played for my benefit...

I DON'T WANT TO MEET THE NEIGHBORS WHO KILLED MY HUSBAND AND SON... NO ONE WHO WASN'T IN THEIR HANDS CAN KNOW WHAT THAT FEAR WAS...

THEY TOOK TWO WOMEN FROM THE MATERNITY WARD AND BROUGHT THEM BACK AT NINE IN THE MORNING. THEY CAME BACK CRY-ING, SCREAM-ING.

AT NIGHT THE SERBS WERE BRINGING PEOPLE— EVEN CHILDREN, WOMEN—AND YOU COULD HEAR SPLASHING IN THE RIVER... THEY SHOT THEM, BUT THEY PREFERRED TO CUT THEIR THROATS.

I heard those scenes in cold, partially burned-out houses and squalid refugee centers, where the walls were scarred by shrapnel, and plastic covered the windows instead of glass.

COURT WILL RECESS FOR HALF AN HOUR.

There were thousands of such scenes, thousands of war criminals to go along with them, but the tribunal has fewer than 30 indictees in custody.

24 of 'em are in this prison.

Neither Bosnian Serb leader Radovan Karadzic nor Bosnian Serb military commander Ratko Mladic, the two "most wanted" suspects, are here. They, too, are charged with genocide...

KARADZIC

MLADIC

J. SACCO 6·98

The tribunal is pursuing more familiar war crimes, like torture and murder, but is breaking new ground in its aggressive investigation of sexual assaults.

Prosecutor Patricia Sellers-Viseur tells me that, prior to these proceedings, war and rape were seen as virtually inseparable...

LIKE MAY SUNSHINE AND FLOWERS, LIKE SALT AND PEPPER.

The longer I'm in The Hague, the more I'm sucked into the courts' orderly deconstruction of some of recent history's foulest moments. I'm fascinated and stupefied by the sheer scope of the arguments, the expert witnesses droning on and on...

BLAH BLAH BLAH FRENCH REVOLUTION BLAH BLAH BLAH REVOLUTIONS OF 1848...

I can't stand the fact that trials are going on simultaneously, that I might be missing something more compelling at the one I'm not at...

BLAH BLAH NATIONAL BLAH

CAN WE DISMISS THIS WITNESS ALREADY?

DISINTEGRA BLAH BLAH

I'm silently cheering judges who are trying valiantly to prod their cases along...

DOES THE COURT NEED TO HEAR WHAT YOUR WITNESS DID FROM HIS BREAKFAST UPON ARRIVING IN BOSNIA TILL THE TIME THE FLAG CAME DOWN WHEN HE LEFT?

The tribunal is emphasizing pretrial management, has added courtrooms, and is petitioning the U.N. for more judges to help pick up the pace.

One of the tribunal's biggest problems, says Nikola Kostich, a former Milwaukee district attorney and a Serb-American defense lawyer, is the perception among some that its prosecution office is biased.

YOU HAVE LIMITED RESOURCES, BUT YOU HAVE TO SHOW RESULTS...

AND I THINK THEY TOOK THE EASY WAY OUT, AND THAT IS TO INVESTIGATE CERTAIN CRIMES AND CHARGE CERTAIN PEOPLE.

AND THE SERBS WERE THE ONES WHO ESSENTIALLY GOT HIT.

He ticks off the names of places where he says Croats and Muslims committed atrocities against Serbs.

Okay, but what about a certain U.N. report that pointed the finger squarely at the Bosnian Serbs?

YOU THINK ITS FINDING THAT SERBS COMMITTED GENOCIDE IN BOSNIA IS INCORRECT?

I THINK THE JURY IS STILL OUT ON WHO DID WHAT TO WHOM IN BOSNIA.

J. SACCO 6-98

The prosecutor's office insists it's building a case against the big fish by frying the smaller fish first. And the tribunal bigwigs don't buy the argument that success should be pegged to any couple of war crimes suspects, no matter how notorious.

The tribunal is dependent on others to apprehend suspects, and so it can't possibly bring every war criminal to justice — and now, with Kosovo erupting, it might have even more war crimes suspects to indict. Still, justice is worth pursuing for its own sake...

TRIBUNAL BUILDING

AND AT LEAST SOMEONE SOMEWHERE IS DRAWING THE LINE — IF ONLY A LEGAL LINE — ON CARNAGE AS WE STUMBLE OUT OF THIS CENTURY OF HORRORS.

But some say this tribunal and the one dealing with Rwanda exist today because of collective Western guilt.

For years we watched the butchery from our living rooms, and now that it's over we've dressed ourselves in robes and decided to do something about it after all.

Pronouncing the word genocide after the fact is a lot safer than stopping it.

It's like Bosnian lawyer Salih Karabdic, who survived the siege of Sarajevo, tells me—

SOMEBODY ORDERED IT, SOMEBODY DID IT, AND SOMEBODY TOLERATED IT.

AND ALL ARE GUILTY.

J. SACCO 6-98

And remember that testicle incident I told you about?

Well, the court determined that the accused, Dusko Tadic, was in the crowd of Bosnian Serbs cheering the scene that day.

They got Tadic on 11 counts, but that wasn't one of them...

ALL RISE!

After all, he was only watching.

The Hague, Notes

Details commissioned "The War Crimes Trials" during the short stint when Art Spiegelman was the magazine's comics editor. I spent slightly less than two weeks at the International Criminal Court for the Former Yugoslavia in The Hague, the Netherlands, in May 1998. For me, the experience of watching the wheels of justice turn, however imperceptibly, was a satisfying cap to the reporting I'd done in Bosnia. Unfortunately, my visit to The Hague ended on a sour note. I had scheduled meetings with the two most important jurists involved in the war crimes trials at the time, Louise Arbour, chief prosecutor for both the former Yugoslavia and the Rwanda tribunals, and Gabrielle Kirk McDonald, president of the former Yugoslavia tribunal and a presiding judge, but they declined to do on-the-record interviews. My conference with them was a bizarre, demeaning episode. McDonald had obtained a number of my comics and had them on the table in front of her. Both she and Arbour had copies of *Details*, too. They insisted they did not object to a story about the tribunal in the comics form per se, but that *Details* magazine, with its glossy photos of spoiled young men and saucily clad women, was not an appropriate forum for an article about such serious matters as war crimes. McDonald read to me some brutal charges from a number of indictments to make her point. Forty-five minutes later, after using every argument I could think of to change their minds, they condescended to do the interviews if I would not quote them or attribute anything to them. In other words, they would talk to me only on background. This is why the last page of "The War Crimes Trials" is weak. It should have been the chief officers of the court who explained the great importance of the work being done at The Hague, not me.

"The War Crimes Trials" appeared in *Details*, September 1998.

THE PALESTINIAN TERRITORIES

HEBRON:
A LOOK INSIDE

An evil electricity crackles through the West Bank town—the sparks that arise when two peoples who hate each other rub together. TIME sent comic journalist **Joe Sacco** there for two weeks. He captured this fresh, provocative view

Colors by Rhea Patton

The taxis bringing us to Hebron can go no farther.

We jump out and make a run for the earthen barricade the Israelis have laid across the main road to hinder the movement of Palestinians.

We're lucky, says my guide Salem, 'cause usually Israeli soldiers are here to harass the people, but who wants to be out in this muck?

There's a slippery dash for taxis on the other side.

By the time we find one with room, 10 minutes later, we're soaked.

But the way to Hebron is now clear.

Hebron is the West Bank's most contentious town, the only one that's divided, the only one with Jewish settlers—who began to establish themselves in the late 1960's—living cheek by jowl with Palestinians.

HEBRON

CONTROLLED BY PALESTINIAN AUTHORITY

CONTROLLED BY ISRAELI MILITARY

H1

H2

In peace process-speak, the Palestinian Authority controls H1, 80% of Hebron; the Israeli military controls the rest, H2.

Let's face it, you have to be ultra-committed to move your family to the heart of a town whose 120,000 residents loathe you, and spokesman David Wilder and the 500 or so other Hebron settlers are just that. Originally from New Jersey, Wilder says it's "perhaps the climax of returning to one's roots" for a Jew to live here.

NEAR THE TEL RUMEIDA SETTLEMENT, H2

THIS IS WHERE ABRAHAM SETTLED...

THIS IS WHERE KING DAVID BEGAN HIS KINGDOM BEFORE HE WENT TO JERUSALEM...

SOMEWHERE UNDER OUR FEET ARE THE ORIGINAL GATES OF HEBRON!

In the Israeli zone, the Tomb of the Patriarchs, Judaism's second holiest site, is underneath the Haram al-Khalil, Islam's fourth holiest place. For 700 years, until Israel occupied the West Bank in 1967, Jews were not allowed to worship inside. "If we were not here," says Wilder, "no Jew would get anywhere close to it."

"It's not a holy site for Jews," insists Nizar Ramadan, a writer associated with Hebron's fundamentalist Islamic movement. He says Israeli-imposed curfews and the other restrictions that often keep Muslim worshippers from the Haram are a "deep discrimination and a new kind of Nazism."

Many Palestinians charge the armed settlers and the soldiers who guard them with abuse and assault. Wilder charges back, "The Arabs are extremely good at lying."

In his view, it's the settlers—in their fortified compounds—who are under siege.

Jews had coexisted with Arabs in Hebron for hundreds of years until shortly after a massacre of 67 Jews by Arabs in 1929, and without the large Israeli army garrison to protect them now—

BEIT HADASSAH COMPOUND, H2

THERE WOULD BE A BLOOD-BATH HERE.

When shots are fired from H1 at the settlers, Israel punishes the 40,000 Palestinians under its control in H2 with a curfew.

The curfew can last months at a time, with breaks of a few hours only every few days.

The curfew prevents Majed Natshe from getting to his sweets shop job in H1. He's lost all his savings, he says.

SOMETIMES I BREAK THE CURFEW TO GO TO WORK...

AND TO GET NECESSARY THINGS FOR THE CHILDREN, DRUGS FOR MY MOTHER.

ALSO, MY WIFE IS PREGNANT. SHE HAS BASIC NEEDS.

He's been shot at three times while breaking the curfew in the back streets of H2, he says.

Wilder says the curfew is the—

PRICE PAID FOR WHAT THEY ARE DOING...

A CURFEW DOESN'T ENDANGER ANYBODY'S LIFE. THE BULLETS THEY ARE SHOOTING AT US DO...

Other bullets, February 1994: Mohammed Abu Ilhalaweh, a father of four, was at the Haram al-Khalil mosque when settler Dr. Baruch Goldstein from nearby Kiryat Arba walked in and killed 29 worshippers.

A gruesome photo on the wall reminds Abu Ilhalaweh of the bullet that paralyzed him that day, but—

THE CASUALTIES OF THE PAST ARE NO LONGER ACKNOWLEDGED.

NOBODY CARES FOR OUR NEEDS BECAUSE THERE ARE NEW CASUALTIES, NEW VICTIMS...

and more than 30 "martyrs" in Hebron so far in this intifadeh.

At the University Graduates Union in H1, I take a sweet from a large bowl and then shake hands with a man whose teenage son was killed by Israeli soldiers three or four days earlier. I'm steered to the front, between rows of men drinking bitter coffee and listening to the exhortations of one speaker after another. Eventually dozens of masked youths march in and face the crowd.

Someone leans over and says, "In America when someone dies, you cry. Here we have a party."

The settlers mourn too. Wilder tells me his daughter's teacher, from another settlement, was killed on a road just outside Hebron. Settlers are sandbagging their windows.

IT'S LIKE LIVING IN A BUNKER.

We're back on the bullets. I'm shown where they've hit settlers' homes.

One bullet entered a bedroom in the Tel Rumeida trailer of Bracha Ben Yitzhak where four of her children were sleeping.

IT'S A MIRACLE THAT NOTHING HAPPENED BECAUSE THE ARABS ARE TRYING TO KILL US.

IT'S WAR HERE.

If it's war, the settlers aren't satisfied with how the Israeli army is conducting it. When you're being shot at "from a particular source night after night, what do you do?" asks Wilder. "You level the house! Very simple to do... And they don't do it."

RESULTS OF ISRAELI FIRE ON THE HARET AL-SHEIKH NEIGHBORHOOD, H1

I tell Wilder I've visited Palestinian homes hit by Israeli fire. Civilians live in them. "But they're shooting from those homes," he insists. If the Israeli army is hitting homes, its spokesman Lieut. Colonel Olivier Rasowicz, claims, "we are very careful and very accurate and only responding to the source of fire."

Yasser Qawasmi's home was raked by Israeli bullets. He denies it was a "source of fire." He says his children now have nightmares.

THIS ONE IS WETTING THE BED...

AND NOW HE'S WETTING HIS CLOTHES TOO, EVEN IN THE DAYTIME.

J. SACCO 1·01

Palestinians in Hebron have been killed in their homes. Fatina al-Fokhouri was wounded.

I WAS CARRYING THE BABY, AND MY HUSBAND GOT THE OTHER THREE KIDS. AS WE TRIED TO GO DOWNSTAIRS, THE FRAGMENTS HIT ME IN THE FOREHEAD AND FLEW OVER MY BODY.

With one of the only English words he knows, her husband Sharif invites me to inspect where Israeli projectiles have punched through the walls.

WEL-COME!

WEL-COME!

Through an interpreter, I ask him if his home, which houses his extended family, was used by gunmen to shoot at the settlers.

WE HAVE 30 CHILDREN IN THIS HOUSE.

I WOULDN'T ALLOW ANYONE TO SHOOT FROM HERE EVEN IF IT WOULD LIBERATE AL-AQSA MOSQUE!

Some of the positions from which Israeli troops fire are forcibly seized Palestinian rooftops in H2.

"We have to be where we have to be to prevent violence from the other side," Rasowicz says.

Israeli soldiers are on Izzi al-Sharabati's roof. He claims they've dumped garbage, urine and excrement on the rest of his house. He says this ceiling is crumbling because soldiers were moving and firing a heavy machine gun on top.

When he complained to the Israelis—

THEY SAID, THANK YOU FOR INFORMING US ABOUT THE DANGER... AND THEY MOVED TO THE OTHER SIDE OF THE ROOF!

WHY DON'T THEY PUT THIS MILITARY POSITION ON THE ROOFS OF THE SETTLERS?

THEY USE US AS A SANDBAG FOR THEIR PROTECTION!

Attached as the settlers are to Hebron, any eventual peace deal will probably mean uprooting them. How? "Military force," predicts Amiram Goldblum, who tracks settlements for the Israeli protest movement Peace Now.

THERE ARE THOSE WHO ARE TRYING TO FORCE US OUT, BE IT VIA POLITICAL MEANS... OR VIOLENCE, HOPING THAT PEOPLE WILL GIVE UP AND LEAVE. WE HAVE NO INTENTION OF DOING THAT.

THIS IS OUR HOME.

Meanwhile, Abu Ilhalaweh says his home is only half a kilometer from the grave of Dr. Baruch Goldstein, who was bludgeoned to death at the scene of the mosque attack. He says on the anniversary of Goldstein's crime and other occasions, settlers gather at the grave.

FROM THE ROAD WE CAN SEE THEM CELEBRATING.

WE HEAR MUSIC FROM UP THERE...

THEY SHOUT, "WHERE ARE YOU, GOLDSTEIN?"

J. SACCO 1-01

GAZA PORTFOLIO

Sabha Abu Mousa searched for her daughter-in-law's two gold bracelets in the rubble of her home, which was demolished by the Israel Defense Forces, in the Khan Younis refugee camp.

Khan Younis refugee camp (left)

The Israeli checkpoint at Abu Houli that divided
Khan Younis and the southern Gaza Strip from
the north (below)

Palestinian fishermen cut off from the Mowasi enclave
(which contained a Jewish settlement bloc) by an Israeli
closure were unable to operate or maintain
their boats and equipment for months.

Boys in Khan Younis followed a truck that
announced the funeral of another "martyr."

Boys from the Khan Younis refugee camp moving up a dune
toward an Israeli jeep. The soldiers taunted the children
("Come on, dogs!" and "Your mother's cunt!") and sometimes
shot at them when they approached too close or threw stones.

The Underground War in Gaza

As the peace process lurches forward (and backward),
towns like Rafah are still at war. A comic-book journalist reports on the battle
over Palestinian tunnels and Israeli bulldozers.

By Joe Sacco

And this man, nicknamed Colonel Pinky, is charged with destroying them. He is the commander of the I.D.F.'s Southern Brigade of the Gaza Strip Division. The I.D.F. claims that "terrorists" sometimes slip through the tunnels, but mainly that they are used for smuggling.

RIGHT NOW MOST OF THE SMUGGLING IS FOR AMMU-NITION.

THE BIG MONEY IS WITH AMMU-NITION.

Colonel Pinky judges his success by the price of a bullet in Rafah. The fewer the tunnels, the higher the price. He says a bullet now costs up to 21 shekels (about $4.50), the highest it's ever been. But that's not good enough, he says. He wants "zero smuggling in my area."

Colonel Pinky is taking me along the narrow Israeli-controlled corridor that divides Palestinian Rafah from Egyptian Rafah, an area so heavily bulldozed that rows of houses that once stood here have been ground down to sand.

More than 860 housing units have been destroyed since the beginning of this intifada, according to the Rafah governorate. The United Nations Relief and Works Agency (Unrwa), which provides aid to Palestinian refugees, puts the number at about 580 — but it counts even a multi-unit structure as a single house.

Colonel Pinky estimates that his bulldozers have demolished between 300 and 400 homes. (An I.D.F. spokesman in Jerusalem later tells me that only "a few dozen" of these were inhabited and suggests that the rest were "abandoned" or unfinished or perhaps sheds for animals.)

Colonel Pinky and I stand behind a 25-foot-high metal wall, which his forces are building as cover from Palestinian sniping. It also goes deep underground to create a barrier to the tunnels.

WE HAVE A LEGAL RIGHT TO DESTROY A HOME WHEN THE HOME IS USED FOR TERROR OPERATIONS.

Houses are destroyed, he says, if they serve as "piers" for tunnels—more than 55 have been discovered so far, according to the I.D.F., sometimes hidden under tile floors or furniture—or if Palestinian militants use them to launch rifle, grenade or anti-tank attacks on his men.

One of his battalion commanders, Lt. Col. Avi, insists:

WE DON'T JUST RANDOMLY DESTROY HOMES.

To demolish a home, he says, he must submit a request that goes all the way up to the "legal adviser of the entire army." (According to the I.D.F., though, this procedure only applies to houses it considers "inhabited.")

J. SACCO 6-03

O.K., I say, let's talk about the destruction of one particular home. It belonged to someone I know—let's call him T.—and it was demolished not four days before, along with a few other dwellings.

The I.D.F. claim that houses demolished are mostly "empty" may be technically accurate, but Palestinians say that it turns the truth on its head. For example, T.'s home was "empty"—but only, he says, because he and his family were chased out by constant Israeli gunfire.

He visited his "empty" house every day, he says, and recently bricked it up so that gunmen couldn't use it.

Colonel Avi knows the houses. He says gunmen used them as cover to shoot at a bulldozer.

YOU CALL THIS A HOME, WE CALL THIS A MILITARY POSITION.

IT'S AN EMPTY HOME, A VACANT HOME THAT NO FAMILY IS LIVING IN.

The Israelis have succeeded in driving a wedge between the people living near the border and the gunmen. Though Palestinians here support the resistance in general, I've heard the gunmen called "useless," even "collaborators," because their ineffective attacks often invite a crushing Israeli response.

I've seen armed men chased off by a man who didn't want them lurking near his house.

Keeping the gunmen out is the "main reason" Fuad stays in his family home near the border despite the entreaties of his parents. The Israelis, he says—

—DON'T NEED AN EXCUSE TO DEMOLISH YOUR HOUSE. BUT THEY CAN USE THE GUNMEN AS A REASON.

While his watchful presence in his home would seem to satisfy the interests of the I.D.F., he says Israeli bullets still hit the house randomly. (I was present during one incident.) Palestinians typically interpret that message as an injunction to flee.

As for the tunnels, the reaction of Sami and his neighbors is precisely what the I.D.F. may have intended all along.

He shows me a tunnel entrance that they had completely blocked up with rubble.

WE DESTROYED THIS HOUSE BECAUSE OF A TUNNEL.

Sami says he and his neighbors "attacked" the smugglers who started this tunnel and chased them away.

He claims a smuggler offered him $60,000 to use his house to build a tunnel—

—AND I REALIZED IT WOULD NOT BE FOR GUNS OR WEAPONS, BUT FOR DRUGS.

I COULD HAVE BEEN A RICH MAN IN ONE NIGHT.

But he says he wants nothing to do with the smugglers. He doesn't want to give the Israelis an excuse to destroy his home.

J. SACCO 6-03

But even so, he can't be sure it will be spared. He says he believes the Israelis are using the issue of tunnels to extend the area they control along the border.

On the edge of Block J, he points to a site where the Israelis found a tunnel—

—150 METERS FROM HERE! SO WHY DID THEY DESTROY THIS WHOLE AREA?

One Palestinian militant I talk to admits that the I.D.F. has been about "90 percent successful" in its efforts to destroy tunnels, but:

NOW WE ARE NOT SO DEPENDENT ON THE TUNNELS AND ON EGYPT.

WITH A FEW MATERIALS AVAILABLE HERE, SUGAR, FOR EXAMPLE, OR FERTILIZER, I CAN CREATE VERY POWERFUL EXPLOSIVE MATERIAL.

He tells me Palestinians are even manufacturing bullets—not as good as "Russian" bullets, he says, but bullets just the same.

I ask Colonel Pinky when the demolitions in Rafah will stop. When "there is no resistance and there is no shooting," he says. "We want the tunnels to be stopped."

All things considered, he characterizes the Israeli response to Palestinian resistance and the tunnels as "gentle, if you can say gentle about something like this." If I wanted to see an army without restraint, he says, I should "go to Chechnya."

Such distinctions may be lost on the 5,300 people Unrwa says have lost their homes here. But T. doesn't seem bitter yet about the destruction of the house that he says he "spent all my life dreaming about."

In fact, after agonizing for weeks as the bulldozers drew nearer, he seems almost relieved now that the deed is done.

YES, BEFORE I HAD HOPE, BUT NOW IT'S FINISHED.

Incidentally, when I returned to Block O to look up the woman who had asked me what I would do in her place, I didn't find her.

The whole row of houses, including hers, was gone.

The Palestinian Territories, Notes

I think of "Hebron: A Look Inside," which appeared in *Time* magazine, as my least successful piece of comics journalism. I cannot blame the senior editor, Joshua Cooper Ramo, who took a chance on comics journalism and supported me every step of the way. Working for that storied publication seemed to freeze me up, and I dispensed with my more typical first-person approach and reverted to the objective, tit-for-tat reporting I'd learned in journalism school. For this reason, I failed to adequately convey the great unfairness of making the free movement of tens of thousands of Palestinians hostage to the considerations of the few hundred militant Jewish settlers.

"Gaza Portfolio" includes both published and unpublished drawings meant to accompany an article my friend and colleague Chris Hedges wrote about Khan Younis, a town and refugee camp in the Gaza Strip. We sold ourselves as a team to Lewis Lapham, editor of *Harper's Magazine* at the time, and he commissioned our weeklong trip to Gaza. Unfortunately, I don't think Mr. Lapham appreciated what I could possibly add to Chris's article with drawings, and he seemed dissatisfied with the ones that showed human faces. I was put off by his second-guessing and almost abandoned the project. As it was, the few drawings published were printed so small as to induce further despair.

I consider "The Underground War in Gaza" a successful project even though, like the *Time* piece about Hebron, I was given only four pages. Representing the *New York Times Magazine* opened doors for me at the Israeli Foreign Press Office, and Israeli spokespersons asked if I would like to spend a day and night with Israel Defense Forces soldiers manning their positions along the Egyptian border. That opportunity allowed me to convey Israeli concerns about weapons smuggling while still questioning the enormous scale of the IDF's home-demolition campaign. Readers of my book *Footnotes in Gaza* might note that the "T" character whose home had just been demolished is Talal, the father of Ashraf, one of that book's main protagonists. Though I have nothing but good things to say about the editor who commissioned the piece, Paul Tough, the story passed through many hands, and there was some effort to get me to comply with the abbreviation commandments of the *New York Times* style guide. Additionally, I had to assure one editor that the background crosshatching on the second panel of the story's last page was not an effort to slip in a lot of little crucifixes.

"Hebron: A Look Inside" appeared in *Time*, March 12, 2001.

Only two of the illustrations shown in "Gaza Portfolio" ("The Khan Younis refugee camp" and "The Israeli checkpoint...") accompanied the article by Chris Hedges, "A Gaza Diary," in *Harper's Magazine*, October 2001; one illustration, "Sabha Abu Mousa...", appeared in a revised form (without the female figure); none of the other illustrations were used.

"The Underground War in Gaza" appeared in the *New York Times Magazine*, July 6, 2003.

THE CAUCASUS

No no!

It's all right!

Easy does it!

No one is sending you back anywhere!

The poor thing has seen my bodyguards, which are required for foreigners traveling here, and thinks they are soldiers who've come to carry her back to the war zone.

Okay!

Everything is under control!

Her name is Zura, and she gets it now.

My translator has explained I come in peace.

In her tent, Zura tells me how she'd fled the war in Chechnya and has been living here as an "Internally Displaced Person" (I.D.P.) in the neighboring Russian republic of Ingushetia, in poor conditions but in safety, when—

I HEARD WOMEN SAYING THAT THE ONES THAT GO BACK TO CHECHNYA WILL BE PROVIDED WITH ACCOMMODATION AND HUMANITARIAN AID.

And Zura bought it.

She did precisely what the Russian authorities wanted her to do. She got on a bus and returned to Chechnya.

In Sernovodsk she was shown her new home, a room in an old technical school. But—

30

Chechnya's most recent anguish began in the early 1990's as the Soviet Union collapsed. The deep grievances of the Chechens against Moscow found radical expression in the person of Jokhar Dudayev, a former loyal Soviet general, who declared Chechnya's independence first thing after ascending to the presidency of the republic in 1991.

Chechnya, which is located in the North Caucasus, had a population of about 1.2 million, one quarter of whom were ethnic Russians. The Russians, who had enjoyed special privileges under the Soviets, made up the majority of the population of the capital Grozny.

Certainly the Russians, but also many Chechens, did not want a total break with the Federation.

Dudayev steered Chechnya—whose independence was never recognized by any country—out of Moscow's political sphere. Civic life deteriorated and poverty was widespread. Government workers went without their salaries.

The kidnap and ransom business, which had historical roots in Chechnya, reasserted itself.

Corrupt Chechens and Russian politicians took advantage of the lack of regulations, customs-free borders, and general chaos to enrich themselves.

Meanwhile, the disputes between Dudayev's supporters and his internal opposition turned deadly.

Dudayev had already dissolved Chechnya's parliament and constitutional court.

As Russia's media stoked long-held prejudices against the Chechens, the political will of Boris Yeltsin's government to negotiate with the problematic Dudayev ebbed.

Under increasing Russian threat, Chechens rallied to Dudayev.

J. SACCO 10-03

Russia was already aiding and arming Chechen groups opposed to Dudayev's administration though Yeltsin still ruled out direct federal military intervention to pull the rebellious republic back into the fold.

WERE WE TO APPLY PRESSURE OF FORCE AGAINST CHECHNYA, THE WHOLE CAUCASUS WOULD RISE UP AND THERE WOULD BE SUCH BLOOD AND TURMOIL THAT NO ONE WOULD FORGIVE US.

IT IS ABSOLUTELY IMPOSSIBLE.

However, newly positioned hardliners in Yeltsin's circle as well as right-wing nationalist rivals pushed the physically diminished Russian president to take harsher measures, which culminated in a military attack in December 1994.

Using overwhelming force, including massive artillery barrages, the Russians devastated Chechen population centers.

J. SACCO 10-03

Shattered Grozny fell to badly bloodied Russian troops after a nearly three-month, block-by-block battle with Chechen fighters. Among the civilian dead—estimated as high as 27,000—were many of the city's ethnic Russians.

The Russian Interior Ministry set up "filtration camps"—supposedly to capture Chechen fighters—which became synonymous with beatings, torture, and murder, and whose chief victims were civilians.

Thousands were "filtered"; 1,500 are still missing.

Poorly trained and fed Russian conscripts were demoralized by a war they didn't understand. If they were wounded, even greviously, their government provided a pittance in compensation; if they were killed, their mothers might have to travel hundreds of miles to identify and retrieve their bodies.

Conscripts sometimes fell victim to robbings and beatings by their ostensible comrades-in-arms, the notorious Interior Ministry contract soldiers—the kontraktniki—often ex-criminals, who preyed mainly on Chechen civilians.

The state of the Russian armed forces was a prescription for robbery, rape, and murder in the areas "liberated" from the "terrorists."

In August 1996, in a surprise offensive, Chechen separatists recaptured Grozny, dealing the Russians a stunning defeat.

J. SACCO 11-03

The Russians agreed to withdraw their troops and to negotiate the republic's final status with the Chechens in five years' time.

The total number of dead during the war was estimated between 30,000 and 80,000. (Dudayev was among those killed.) More than 320,000 had fled their homes to become I.D.P.'s.

A new Chechen president, Aslan Maskhadov, formerly chief of staff of Chechen forces, could not stop the post-war republic from descending into further lawlessness and economic chaos.

A number of dramatic events in 1999 deepened the crisis. First, two warlords led a raid from Chechnya into the neighboring Russian republic of Daghestan, where they declared an independent Islamic territory. (Their "other" motives are the subject of some speculation.)

The raid precipitated the reemergence of the Moscow hawks. Yeltsin picked Vladimir Putin, the counterintelligence chief, to be Russia's prime minister.

Putin lost little time in confronting the warlords with force.

Next, a series of bomb blasts killed hundreds of Russians, including scores in Moscow apartment buildings.

Though serious questions remain about the mysterious explosions, Moscow — which was itself implicated — was quick to blame the Chechens.

With popular backing, Putin launched a second war on Chechnya in 1999. Federal forces took Grozny again after severe bombardments and house-to-house fighting and with seeming disregard for civilian losses.

Russian troops have managed to occupy most of Chechnya thereafter, but the separatists still operate and exact a toll.

Large bombs —including suicide bombs —have brought death not just to Russian soldiers and their local supporters, but also to innocent bystanders in places like Grozny's markets.

Those who remain in Chechnya must also contend with the danger of landmines, the imposition of curfews, and the certainty of power and water cuts.

And into this chaos, Russia pretends that it is perfectly safe for people like Zura to return and start their lives again.

J. SACCO 11.03

Or that it is safe for Raisa, who fled to Ingushetia after her husband was killed, and must now raise five children alone...

THIS BOY IS ONLY EIGHT YEARS OLD AND HE HAS HEART PROBLEMS.

HE FALLS UNCONSCIOUS WHEN HE SEES RUSSIAN SOLDIERS.

THE RUSSIANS COME AND TURN EVERYTHING UPSIDE-DOWN, AND THEY INSULT AND ABUSE PEOPLE.

THEY SHOUT AT WOMEN AND CHILDREN.

THEY TAKE EVERYTHING THEY WANT FROM THE HOUSES.

T.V.'S, CARPETS, CLOTHES.

IN ONE DAY THEY CAME FIVE TIMES.

THEY CAME MAYBE 40 TIMES ALL TOGETHER.

Or that it is safe for Zalva, who accompanies her sons daily through the many Russian checkpoints on the way to Grozny, where they study, and then back to Ingushetia, where they've taken refuge.

JUST LAST WEEK A RUSSIAN SOLDIER GRABBED THE SLEEVE OF MY 16 YEAR OLD AND WANTED TO TAKE HIM OUT OF THE CAR.

HE WET HIMSELF.

J. SACCO 11-03

37

But despite all the stories that filter in from Chechnya, despite what they know themselves, some I.D.P.'s still try to go back. Some feel their conditions in Ingushetia are too miserable to endure any longer.

Back in Sputnik camp, I meet Larisa and her sister Fatima, who tells me—

MY TENT WAS IN TERRIBLE CONDITIONS, ESPECIALLY WHEN IT RAINED.

I COULDN'T GET A NEW TENT.

SO WHEN EVERYONE PUT IN AN APPLICATION [FOR CHECHNYA], I PUT MINE IN.

EMERCOM, the Russian agency responsible for emergencies and natural disasters, promised her "a room with all the conveniences," and was so pleased when she agreed to move back that it sent a small truck to take her and her kids to Gudarmes, Chechnya.

The small room she was given was clean, she says, but came without gas or heat or a functioning sink. The toilet was outside.

Worse, the humanitarian aid EMERCOM doles out in Chechnya— it has stopped doing so in Ingushetia— is a tiny fraction of what her family needs.

She says the monthly ration per person is one can of beef, one tin of condensed milk, one kilo of sugar, one kilo of rice, and one packet of tea.

I repeat: per month.

And about that canned beef—

THE QUALITY IS SO BAD WE CAN'T EAT IT.

J. SACCO 12-03

38

II. EVERY 50 YEARS

Asset lives in an abandoned milk factory called M.T.F. Karabulak.

Her family has three cows, which are out to pasture.

WE HAD CATTLE BEFORE THE FIRST WAR, BUT THEY WERE KILLED BY SOLDIERS.

AND THIS TIME WE BROUGHT THE CATTLE WITH US, NOT SO MUCH FOR US, BUT OUT OF PITY FOR THEM.

WE DIDN'T WANT THEM TO BE SHOT.

Asset knows full well that the recent wars are in a long series of historical disasters that have overtaken the Chechen people ever since the Russian empire pushed its way into the North Caucasus in the 1700's.

The rebellious Chechens—demonized as bandits by the Russians—were never fully subdued despite dozens of military expeditions to bring them to heel.

In the Soviet era, the Chechens resisted Stalin's agricultural collectivization. In one day in 1937 the Red Army rounded up and shot 14,000 Chechens.

But the worst was to come.

J. SACCO 12-03

In a small room built for her by her sons, Asset sighs—

THIS REPEATS EVERY CENTURY, EVERY 50 YEARS.

VAINAKH* PEOPLE SHOULD SCATTER ALL OVER THE WORLD BECAUSE IF THEY GATHER IN ONE PLACE THEY ARE EASILY ANNIHILATED.

Asset is thinking back to a day in February 1944 and the defining catastrophe in her people's history.

I WAS SIX YEARS OLD, AND I REMEMBER QUITE A LOT.

"On the previous evening, the soldiers called all the men to a meeting.

"They took them to a storage building and locked them in.

"My mother had gone to the market to buy wool, and she couldn't reach our house because the soldiers had encircled the village and wouldn't let her pass through.

"Only in the morning did she reach our family. I remember her running and screaming and carrying that bag of wool.

J. SACCO 1·04

*VAINAKH: THE NAME GIVEN TO THE CLOSELY RELATED CHECHEN AND INGUSH PEOPLE AS A WHOLE.

41

This was Stalin's final solution for the Chechens. whom he would later accuse of collaborating with the invading Nazis. His army had herded every Chechen and Ingush man, woman, and child onto trains— 12,000 carriages had been assembled for the task — and deported them en masse to Kazakhstan.

"It must have been a 17- or 18-day journey.

"At stops, young people ran for the food that was prepared at the stations. But the stops were short and too many people would be in line. And if the family didn't have plates, they didn't get food.

"When people had to go to the toilet they weren't allowed to go far from the carriage. When the train stopped they had to get off and do it right there.

"If someone crawled under the train to get to the other side, a soldier would beat them.

J. SACCO 1-04

43

"When we arrived in Kazakhstan we were met by people with horses, oxen, and camels...from there we were taken to different villages.

"We lived together with a Kazakhai family and other Chechen families...

"My father was arrested soon after we arrived. They said he was a kulak.*"

"He joined the family again four and a half years later.

"My mother gave birth to a baby daughter, and they both died. My mother died a year after the stillbirth. She was in bed for a year."

Most of the deportees were forced to fend for themselves in the unfamiliar landscape. Within five years one quarter of them—145,000 people—had died from cold and hunger.

J. SACCO 5-04

*KULAK: DEROGATORY TERM SOVIETS APPLIED TO PROSPEROUS PEASANTS.

What had been the republic of Chechen-Ingushetia ceased to exist. It was divided up and its parts transferred to neighboring Soviet republics. Russians and Daghestanis were settled in Chechen homes, and the Soviets systematically set out to destroy Chechnya's cultural heritage.

The Chechens were rehabilitated by Khrushchev in 1957 and allowed to return to their homeland, which was reconstituted.

But they were never compensated for their losses or for the brutality meted out against them.

The common experience of the deportations has left its indelible mark upon the Chechens.

If Asset were to compare that time to this, she says it was worse then.

DUE TO THE HUMANITARIAN ORGANIZATIONS THE PEOPLE NOW DON'T KNOW WHAT HUNGER IS.

Asset sometimes returns to her hometown in Chechnya to pick up her modest monthly pension if her son can't make the trip for her.

Sometimes she visits her old house. I ask her to describe what she sees...

"I see a destroyed place," she tells me, "abandoned, overgrown with weeds."

47

III. THE CAMPS

Let's say you are a Chechen running from the war.

You get on a bus for Ingushetia's capital, Nazran, and you arrive some hours later with only the clothes on your back.

Where to then?

I ask Hazhan, who faced just such a proposition two weeks ago. She fled Chechnya with five children right after recovering from a bullet wound that had cut through her intestines in 13 places.

I WAS AT THE BUS STATION, AND I ASKED THE PEOPLE IF THEY KNEW A PLACE WHERE I COULD STAY THE NIGHT WITH MY CHILDREN.

And someone directed Hazhan to this automotive repair yard, Logovaz, in downtown Nazran, which has been partially given over to I.D.P.'s. It's a crowded facility with tents filling up the ground in front of the garages, but a few people made space for her inside a former storeroom.

Including her and her five children, about 15 people live here now, she says.

I DON'T WANT TO BE A BURDEN, AND THAT'S WHY I HAVE TO FIND A PLACE FOR MYSELF.

Hazhan has done what so many Chechens have had to do, namely figure out accommodation for themselves. There is no one to "meet and greet" the I.D.P.'s that trickle into Ingushetia, no central agency that directs them to this room or that tent.

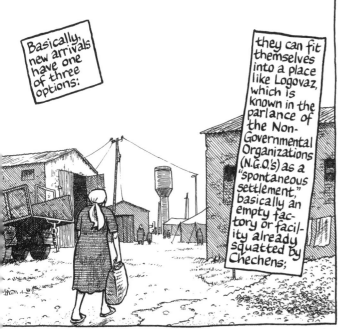

Basically, new arrivals have one of three options:

they can fit themselves into a place like Logovaz, which is known in the parlance of the Non-Governmental Organizations (N.G.O.'s) as a "spontaneous settlement," basically an empty factory or facility already squatted by Chechens;

they can join one of the tent camps;

or, if they can afford to, they can rent a room or house for themselves.

Many opt to rent when they first arrive in Ingushetia, but they move to the squalid spontaneous settlements or overcrowded tent camps when their money runs out.

N.G.O.'s have struggled to provide the settlements and camps with basic facilities like toilets and baths and access to water, gas, and electricity.

I decide to check out living conditions by making a tour of as many I.D.P. sites as I can.

My sampling starts at the Plievo chicken farm.

They have the same trouble with vermin at Tanzila, a spontaneous settlement in Nazran.

One lady is hoping I can do something about it.

CAN YOU HELP ME GET RID OF THE RATS?

Her name is Zainap, and she lives near one of the camp toilets, which means her problem is particularly acute.

THE WHOLE NIGHT THEY RUN OVER THE ROOF.

SEVERAL TIMES THEY'VE COME THROUGH HOLES, AND MY HUSBAND KILLED THEM WITH A STICK.

For Yaha, mice and cockroaches are the least of her worries.

She lives in the sprawling ZhBi cement factory on the road from Nazran to Karabulak, which houses scores of I.D.P.'s.

Parts of the plant are still operating.

Trucks race up and down carrying loads from a gravel pit.

The dangers in this settlement abound. Yaha's eldest, Ilias, age 15, was killed when he touched an unprotected high-voltage cable.

WHENEVER I GO TO GET WATER I SEE THE PLACE WHERE MY SON DIED.

Her husband and a daughter were killed in Chechnya.

Yaha lives in this drafty former workshop with her five surviving children.

At the same settlement, some people motion me over to several large metal rings that open on an empty underground water reservoir.

One woman tells me that children playing here have fallen into the pit on a number of occasions.

She produces her four-year-old nephew.

He fell down there twice!

WERE YOU HURT?

NO I WASN'T!

Lucky kid! It's a 12-foot drop at least.

J. SACCO 9.04

Now, what about the tent camps?

Some of the biggest, like Sputnik, are situated in the middle of nowhere, close to the Chechen border.

At Sputnik, lines of toilets ring the tents or are set off a couple of dozen meters from the dusty roads.

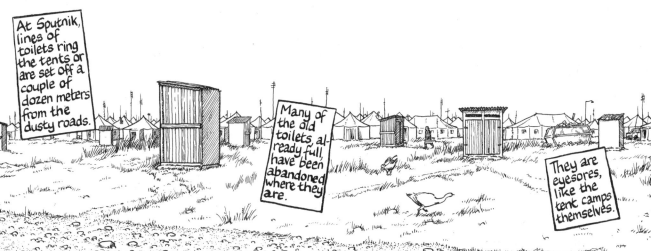

Many of the old toilets, already full, have been abandoned where they are.

They are eyesores, like the tent camps themselves.

It is the tent camps—the most visible reminder that the war in Chechnya is not over—which most embarrass the Russian government. The Russians make bellicose statements about removing them, while promising the I.D.P.'s better facilities elsewhere.

Says Tamara, a resident of Iman camp:

THEY SAID THEY WOULD BRING BULLDOZERS AND TRACTORS TO SMASH ALL THE TENTS...

AND BRING POLICE TO BEAT PEOPLE WITH RUBBER STICKS.

J. SACCO 7.04

As it was, Esita moved from one overcrowded tent to another, four times in one year. Finally she had enough, and this place—with a whole room for herself and her family—looked mighty good.

THERE IS NO ONE TO SCOLD THE CHILDREN.

I CAN COOK WHEN I WANT TO.

I DON'T HAVE TO LOSE MY DIGNITY IN FRONT OF SOMEONE ELSE.

Lyuba and Aslambeck, also recent transplants from Iman, live with their children in spacious rooms nearby.

TO MY MIND, IT'S BETTER TO HAVE ROOF AND WALLS INSTEAD OF A TENT.

IT WAS COLD, AND THE TENT HADN'T BEEN WINTERIZED.

But, Lyuba admits, she feared they would be moved from Iman anyway.

A REPRESENTATIVE OF THE MIGRATION SERVICES KEPT COMING AND SAYING THE TENTS WERE TO BE REMOVED.

TELL THE TRUTH.

THEY THREATENED TO BRING BULLDOZERS AND FLATTEN THAT PLACE.

J. SACCO 7.04

IV. ZARA

Zara lives in one of a series of disused cowsheds at a former milk factory in Altiyevo.

Did I say "disused"?

Actually, there's a pen at the back of Zara's shed—a dozen feet from where people live—that houses cattle brought over from Chechnya by I.D.P.'s.

The smell of dung in the corridor between the windowless cubicles overpowers the smell I'm used to in places like this—gas.

Watch your step though!

Exposed gas pipes lead off the main and cross your path.

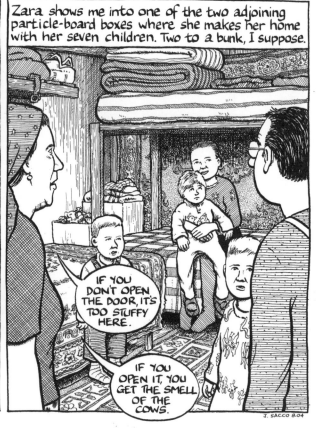

Zara shows me into one of the two adjoining particle-board boxes where she makes her home with her seven children. Two to a bunk, I suppose.

IF YOU DON'T OPEN THE DOOR, IT'S TOO STUFFY HERE.

IF YOU OPEN IT, YOU GET THE SMELL OF THE COWS.

J. SACCO 8·04

It's stuffy all right, but as cheery as a room in a cowshed can get. She's hung up carpets on the wall.

THIS PLACE IS DAMP, AND THEY MAKE IT BETTER.

THEY MAKE IT COSY.

Zara bought these rooms for 4,000 rubles from the previous owner, who built them himself from donated material and charged her for his labor.

She's just paid another 3,000 on a room for her husband, who only escaped from Chechnya last month, and his two nephews, who were orphaned in the first war.

His name is Issa.

He is watchful but sits passively while Zara does the talking.

He has been tortured, she says.

Detained for six months.

Tortured.

As if on cue, he hikes up his trouser leg. The Russians shot him, you see. He was sitting with his hands on his head and they put a bullet through his ankle.

He yanks up his pullover.

You see the welts?

They heated up a knife and cut him with it over and over.

HE ALMOST WENT INSANE.

HE DIDN'T RECOGNIZE HIS OWN FAMILY WHEN HE WAS RELEASED.

HE BEAT THE CHILDREN.

HE BEAT OUR OWN DAUGHTER SO SEVERELY THAT SHE ALSO HAS MENTAL PROBLEMS.

ONCE HE TIED MY HANDS TOGETHER AND MY FEET TOGETHER AND WAS GOING TO SLAUGHTER ME WITH A KNIFE.

J. SACCO 8-04

HE'S BETTER NOW.

In the second war, Zara was wounded and fled Grozny with the children after their home was completely destroyed. Issa, whose passport and papers had been lost, remained behind. Without identification, he was unwilling to risk the journey to Ingushetia and another arrest by the Russians. He didn't even dare step out of his brother's house.

"Almost every week I would go to Chechnya to bring him food," Zara tells me. "I had to take him food from my family's humanitarian ration or he would have died of hunger.

"When I couldn't go for three months, I found him eating unground wheat and drinking sunflower oil."

She decided to chance getting him out. She paid a taxi driver 1,000 rubles – $33 – to find a route around the many Russian checkpoints to Ingushetia.

And now he is here with them...

an invalid.

But if he cannot work, and if you are responsible for him, for his two nephews, and for your seven children, how do you make ends meet?

SOMETIMES I'M SURPRISED MYSELF.

BECAUSE GOD HELPS ME, I MANAGE.

Yes, yes, there's God...

J. SACCO 9-04

and there's humanitarian relief, too.

Relatives and a kind woman named Raisa helped when Zara didn't have a ruble to her name.

Someone else gave her two mattresses and a blanket for the children.

Now she works in the market, she says... but it's hard.

EVERY-THING IS HARD.

IF MY CHILDREN ARE SICK, I CAN'T AFFORD TO TAKE THEM TO A DOCTOR.

I HAVE TO LET THEM GET OVER THEIR ILLNESS THEM-SELVES.

When I get up to leave, Zara lets her defenses down. She asks if there's anything I can do.

NO, I DON'T WANT YOUR OWN MONEY.

BUT COULD YOU ASK SOME-ONE AT AN N.G.O. TO HELP ME?

I never know what to say to someone who thinks I have connections with important officials who can tend to her special case.

Two days later I run into Zara on her way to work.

DO YOU NEED A LIFT?

WHAT HOURS DO YOU WORK?

I START WORK-ING AT THE KIOSK AT SEVEN THIS EVENING, AND I FINISH AT TEN.

J. SACCO 9-04

59

I think she means ten at night.

NO...

TEN IN THE MORNING.

Ten in the morning?

Are you kidding?

NO, AND THEN I WORK UNTIL NOON AT ANOTHER PLACE SELLING BIS- CUITS AND CAKE.

But that's a total of 17 hours!

HOW CAN YOU DO THAT? WHEN DO YOU SLEEP?

YESTERDAY I SLEPT ONLY TWO HOURS. IT'S JUST TOO NOISY.

SOMETIMES I FALL ASLEEP AT THE KIOSK, AND A CUSTOMER COMES AND WAKES ME.

Our con- versation is cut short 'cause here we are.

We drop Zara off.

She's thanking us.

We've saved her a long walk.

J. SACCO 9.04

V. GETTING BY

Remember Hazhan, who arrived at Logovaz just two weeks ago with five kids and a bullet wound? Well, like many I.D.P.'s I talk to, she fled the war with nothing but the shirt on her back.

I ONLY HAVE WHAT I'M WEARING.

REALLY.

I'M NOT SAYING THAT TO GET SYMPATHY.

She says her children don't have a change of clothes either.

BUT THEN HOW DO YOU DO THEIR LAUNDRY?

"I do the washing when the children are asleep," she says. "I'm lucky I have good neighbors who give me soap and detergent.

"The other women have given me some shoes for the children."

Like most all recent Chechen arrivals, Hazhan must rely on the generosity of those who have already settled into their lives here as I.D.P.'s.

The most important thing her new roommates have done for Hazhan is help her get on the Danish Refugee Council list.

Of all the lists, this is the one that matters most.

Everyone on it is ensured a basic monthly ration of food— flour, oil, sugar, and iodized salt.

It's up to international aid agencies to tend to the basic needs of the I.D.P.'s

The Russian government stopped providing soup and bread to the I.D.P.'s in 2001.

J. SACCO 9.04

The international aid groups hand out building materials, tents, and necessities like stoves, but there is never enough to go around.

Hadet, who lives at the abandoned milk factory at Altiyevo, tells me—

RECENTLY AN AGENCY CAME AROUND DISTRIBUTING MATTRESSES, BUT WE WERE NOT ON THE LIST AND DIDN'T GET EVEN ONE.

What about these other possessions, these pans, these buckets?

THE THINGS WE HAVE ARE PRESENTS FROM OUR DAUGHTER.

Hadet, her husband, and their three grandchildren must share two single matresses between them.

Hadet must supplement whatever is given out.

When I meet her, she was getting ready to walk to nearby fields to collect small potatoes that Ingush farmers hadn't bothered to dig up.

Most I.D.P.'s try to earn money in some way or other. Hazhan, for example, has already sold her gold rings, earrings, and bracelets. One of her children now helps out by selling cassettes in the market while Hazhan washes floors.

I HAVE HIGHER EDUCATION...

I WAS AN ACCOUNTANT, A TECHNICAL INSTITUTE GRADUATE...

AND I'M FULL OF ENERGY.

I THINK I WILL OVERCOME THIS.

UNFORTUNATELY, MY HEALTH ISN'T GOOD.

J. SACCO 9.04

VI. ZAMANI

Zamani lives in a cowshed at the abandoned Nasir-Kort milk factory.

She isn't well.

She barely leaves her stuffy particle-board room, which is a bit more than six feet square and just over six feet high.

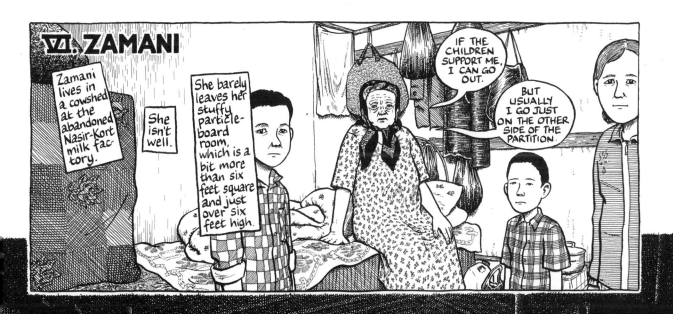

IF THE CHILDREN SUPPORT ME, I CAN GO OUT.

BUT USUALLY I GO JUST ON THE OTHER SIDE OF THE PARTITION.

On the other side of the partition is an unlit corridor that divides rows of similar box rooms made by I.D.P.'s from the same particle board or mud bricks.

Referring to the Russians, Zamani says...

SOMETIMES THEY CUT THE ELECTRICITY.

SOMETIMES THEY CUT THE GAS.

IF THEY CUT THE GAS, WE HAVE NOTHING ELSE TO HEAT THE ROOM.

FORTUNATELY, WE HAVE CANDLES.

Zamani has lived here for two months. Her husband died of natural causes in Chechnya. Zamani refused to flee to Ingushetia before the mourning period ended...

and then—

"—a rocket hit our house and my daughter was killed, and I was wounded in the head by shrapnel."

"Actually, my daughter wasn't killed immediately.

"Her spine was broken.

J. SACCO 10-04

"She was taken to hospital, but then the Russian troops closed the village. No one was allowed in or out for ten days.

"On the 11th day I was able to visit her.

"I told the doctor I'd come again the next day, but after I left the hospital she died."

Her other daughter, Samani, traveled from her home in Nagrovsky, elsewhere in the Russian Federation, to bring Zamani here. Samani then collected her children and moved in with her mother.

Wait!

You left your home in Nagrovsky for a cowshed?

I'M USED TO DIFFICULTIES, AND INCONVENIENCES DO NOT SCARE ME.

MY HUSBAND REMAINED BECAUSE HERE HE WOULDN'T BE ABLE TO FIND A JOB.

AND HE DIDN'T WANT TO GET INVOLVED IN ALL THIS WAR STUFF.

She says she's happier here among her own people where her children can be raised with Chechen values.

"I don't like the behavior of the young boys and girls in Russia. They smoke, they drink, they could kiss, and this doesn't coincide with Chechen traditions and culture."

J. SACCO 10-04

But there was something else...

SINCE THE WAR BEGAN THE ATTITUDE OF THE RUSSIANS HAS CHANGED GREATLY TOWARD THE CHECHENS.

THE ATTITUDE HAS BECOME MORE AGGRESSIVE TOWARD THE SCHOOL CHILDREN.

OF COURSE THERE WERE GOOD PEOPLE THERE, TOO, BUT THE BAD ONES PREVAILED.

So now Samani lives here with her mother and four children.

They have two mattresses between them.

I BROUGHT NOTHING FROM HOME.

EVERYTHING WAS DESTROYED, BURNED.

IT WAS A BIG ROCKET.

BUT DID YOU AT LEAST BRING OUT A COAT?

I DIDN'T BRING A COAT.

I DON'T HAVE CLOTHES HERE.

ONLY WHAT PEOPLE GAVE ME... PEOPLE ALWAYS HELP EACH OTHER.

So what's the most important possession you own now?

I HAVE THIS STOVE, BUT IT DOESN'T BELONG TO ME. SOMEONE LENT IT.

But what about income, Zamani? Don't you have a pension?

I'M GETTING A PENSION, BUT I'M AFRAID TO TAKE IT.

Can't your daughter go to Chechnya to collect it for you?

I DON'T LET HER.

I'M SCARED FOR HER.

IF SOMETHING HAPPENS TO HER, WHAT WILL I DO WITH THE CHILDREN?

J. SACCO 10-04

I CAN'T RECOVER FROM THE FEAR I HAD WHEN I HEARD THE PLANES. USUALLY, EVERY DAY, THE PLANES FLEW ABOVE THE HOUSE.

I CAN'T SLEEP SINCE MY DAUGHTER DIED. BUT, STILL, IT'S QUIETER HERE...

I'M SORRY I AM CRYING.

IT'S MUCH BETTER HERE THAN IN CHECHNYA.

I APOLOGIZE AGAIN FOR CRYING. MY DAUGHTER WAS VERY GOOD TO ME.

I change the subject. I ask about the deportation of 1944, which Zamani barely remembers.

THIS IS WORSE, MUCH WORSE.

NOW THE RUSSIAN TROOPS KILL PEOPLE WHILE THEY ARE DRIVING, WHILE THEY ARE TRYING TO FLEE THE WAR.

THEY CUT PEOPLE'S FLESH WHILE THEY ARE STILL ALIVE.

THEY DRIVE THEIR TANKS AND A.P.C.'S OVER THE WOUNDED.

I WANT TO SHOW YOU A PHOTOGRAPH OF MY DAUGHTER.

J. SACCO 10·04

WHAT REFUGEES?

RUSSIA SWEEPS THE CHECHENS UNDER THE RUG

by Joe Sacco © 2002

Every so often, with a straight face, Russia's President Putin declares that the fight to keep Chechnya in the Russian Federation is won.

The bloody hostage crisis in a Moscow theater put the lie to that, as do the comments of Zara Ozdiyeva, and others like her, who continue to cross the border from Chechnya into the neighboring Russian republic of Ingushetia....

WE WERE ESCAPING DEATH.

WE LEFT OUR HOME AND EVERYTHING WE HAD THERE...

IN CHECHNYA WE HAD TO SLEEP UNDER THE BEDS BECAUSE OF THE BULLETS AND SHELLS.

My dear Zara! You are spoiling Putin's image as the man who brought order to the North Caucasus!

And so to bring reality in line with fantasy, Putin wants you and the 110,000 other "Internally Displaced Persons" (IDP's) either packed back to Chechnya — where Russia's brutalities against civilians are notorious in its "anti-terrorist war"— or scattered to less visible sites than this eyesore of a tent camp.

No camps means no refugees! No refugees means the situation is under control!

And in a tent camp called Iman an IDP named Tamara relates the threat made during a personal visit by Russia's First Deputy Head of Migration Services in September.

THEY SAID THEY WOULD BRING BULLDOZERS AND TRACTORS TO SMASH ALL THE TENTS.

Haron Elzhurkayev, the commandant of a small refugee settlement in an abandoned chicken farm, describes a heated meeting between camp leaders and a Chechen politician who owed his allegiance to Moscow...

HE TRIED TO THREATEN US SAYING, IF WE THINK THERE WON'T BE "CLEANSING" OPERATIONS HERE, WE ARE WRONG.

For months the word has filtered down that the clock is ticking for the Chechens who've found sanctuary in Ingushetia.

CASPIAN SEA

RUSSIAN FEDERATION

INGUSHETIA

GROZNY

CHECHNYA

NAZRAN

NAZRAN TO MOSCOW APPROX. 1000 MILES

0   50
|———|
MILES

GEORGIA

A 20-step plan signed in May by Ingush and pro-Russian Chechen representatives, under Russia's helpful direction, states plainly that the camps are to be removed and the IDP's sent back to Chechnya.

The Caucasus, Notes

"Chechen War, Chechen Women" was included in a series of books packaged together under the title *I Live Here* to benefit Amnesty International. The immensely good-hearted actress Mia Kirshner had assembled a diverse group of writers, artists, photographers, and designers to tackle human rights issues around the world that were receiving little attention at the time. She asked me to accompany her to Ingushetia to meet refugees from the war in neighboring Chechnya, and she paid for my flights, my accommodations, and our bodyguards. Bodyguards were a requirement for foreigners traveling in the area (to discourage kidnapping) and were probably there to report our movements to the authorities as well. We had three bodyguards each, and this amused me to no end. ("I'm sitting around with three personal bodyguards, sneering at journalists who've only hired two," I wrote in my journal.) But the entourage of bodyguards seemed to upset some of the traumatized Ingush refugees we approached, as I detail at the beginning of the story. I took to bringing only the most easygoing bodyguard with me into the camps and insisting the others wait in the car. Among the people who truly need protection in the Caucasus are the courageous staff members of Memorial, a local human rights organization, without whose help Mia and I could not have done our work. Memorial personnel have become targets of those who do not appreciate the exposure of ongoing human rights violations in the post-Soviet nations.

"What Refugees?" is an editorial, and it is perhaps the only occasion in which I tried to respond to a real-time situation immediately. It was completed for the *Boston Globe*'s Ideas section for deputy editor Jenny Schuessler within a few weeks of my leaving Ingushetia.

"Chechen War, Chechen Women" appeared in *I Live Here*, published by Pantheon Books, 2008.

"What Refugees?" appeared in the *Boston Globe*, November 17, 2002.

IRAQ

COMPLACENCY KILLS

by Joe Sacco © 2005

"When I'm on the road," says Sgt. Dance, commander of Mobile Assault Platoon (MAP) 4, explaining his policy toward Iraqi drivers here, "you're not on the road."

And so as we race to check on a report of some vehicles linking up in the middle of nowhere, the oncoming traffic had better get out of the way!

Lance Cpl. Janigo, binoculars pressed to his face, yells—

SINGLE!

—and Lance Cpl. Battles, the driver, flashes his lights until the startled Iraqi swerves off the road.

A single Iraqi in a car fits their profile of a suicide bomber, and our Humvee barely whizzes by that potential threat when two more cars come flying our way from under a bridge.

There's no time for Lance Cpl. Janigo to adjust his binoculars or for Lance Cpl. Battles to flash his lights!

Sgt. Dance screams—

GET 'EM OFF THE ROAD!

GET 'EM OFF THE ROAD!

—and Lance Cpl. Clark fires a burst across the front of the first car!

Both vehicles veer to a stop, and I catch a glimpse of a man with a moustache as we punch by.

J. SACCO 1-05

A few minutes later we reach the suspicious group of cars, which turns out to be a funeral procession.

"The bad guys don't usually congregate in vehicles on the side of the road," says Sgt. Dance, who was skeptical all along. "It's painfully obvious."

And to the bereaved he adds—

OUR SYMPATHIES ARE WITH YOU.

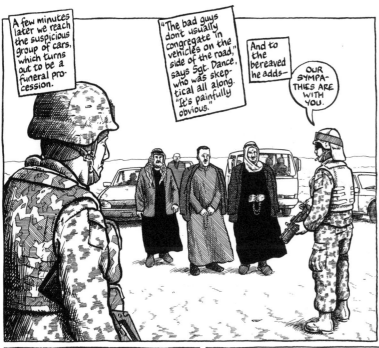

The primary mission of Sgt. Dance and the MAPs of the Weapons Company of the 1st Battalion, 23rd Marine Regiment is to keep the roads between Haditha and Hit open to U.S. convoys.

Their adversaries are insurgents whose chief weapons are roadside and vehicle-borne bombs and land mines. Twisted bits of car metal, charred patches of ground, and craters attest to the violence they've dished out to the Americans.

The Marines of the 1/23, who are nearly all Texan reservists, run most of their road patrols in this stretch of western Iraq from the functioning ten-story high Haditha Dam on the Euphrates River.

The stairwells reek of sulfur, but the Marines are otherwise smothered in home comforts: They enjoy a well-equipped weight room,

football on the chow hall's big-screen TV, and 24-hour internet connections to their wives and mothers.

I'm bunking on the fifth deck in a room full of officers where Lt. Crabtree, the battalion adjutant, projects a movie on the wall every night and dispenses snacks from an endless supply of pooled care packages.

The room's coffee aficionado is the commander of the engineering platoon, Capt. Kuniholm, and once I ask what motivated a married, liberal, business-owning Ph.D. student like himself to join the reserves knowing full well he would be sent to Iraq. A sense of duty, he answers.

Also— YOU SHOULDN'T DISCOUNT THE SPIRIT OF WHITE, UPPER-MIDDLE CLASS ADVENTURISM.

Almost discordantly in this cocooned world of X-Boxes and Maxim magazines, a sign on the second deck reminds the Marines of the MAPs heading down to their Humvees that—

COMPLACENCY KILLS

J. SACCO 1-08

77

But even these veterans are lulled by the quiet of the last few weeks, and, on a hilltop buffeted by cold winds, they break the tedium of another 13-hour patrol with a hot dinner of canned ravioli and chicken soup.

Then... in the distance... a massive blast!

THAT THING SOUNDED LIKE A FUCKING S.V.B.I.E.D.*! THAT THING WAS BIG!

GO! GO! GO!

* SUICIDE VEHICLE-BORNE IMPROVISED EXPLOSIVE DEVICE

Everyone's wound up like I haven't seen them before!

Everyone aims a weapon at the Iraqi cars, which pull over pronto!

We reach a group of Humvees from another mission.

A roadside bomb went off between two vehicles in an area the Marines I'm with had checked out in the morning.

One Marine, Lance Cpl. Knepper, has shrapnel in his right arm.

Lance Cpl. Knepper, accompanied by his platoon medic, Doc Perez, climbs into our highback, which races for Haditha Dam escorted by the Humvees of MAP 2.

WHEN'S THIS MORPHINE GOING TO KICK IN?

As soon as the injured Marine is passed off to the Battalion Aid Station, Sgt. Johnson and Sgt. Cantu ask each other the same question: How did the insurgents place a bomb under so many Marine noses?

DIDN'T YOU SWEEP THAT AREA?

WE DID SWEEP THAT AREA.

I SWEPT IT!

J. SACCO 2-08

78

We reach the stopped car, a taxi.

The platoon's other Humvees join us and take up position.

No one's in the mood for games.

THEY'RE WAVING A WHITE FUCKING FLAG!

The Marines motion the Iraqis out of their vehicle. Sgt. Cantu and Lance Cpl. Ledesma, who has taken a crash course in Arabic, dismount and approach them.

The passengers turn out to be a family.

Their taxi has broken down.

We find another hilltop.

The crew begins to unwind.

One or two of them will catch some sleep.

But not Sgt. Cantu.

He's beating himself up about the bomb that went off earlier.

IT HAPPENED ON OUR WATCH.

WE WERE SUPPOSED TO SECURE THE AREA.

THERE'S ALWAYS MORE WE COULD HAVE DONE.

EVERYWHERE YOU LOOK YOU SEE 'COMPLACENCY KILLS.'

IT'S BULL-SHIT—

—UNTIL IT HAPPENS.

A patrol or two later, I become impatient with the cat-and-mouse game in the desert.

Frankly, it seems we will never see a mouse...

and if we don't

do I have a story?

So I join the Marines' Small Craft Company on one of its river sorties from the dam.

I'm hoping to find some real action out on the Euphrates.

80

But no such luck.

All we do is intercept a pair of Iraqis who've come too close to the dam.

GET OUT OF HERE!

GET THE FUCK OUT!

Afterwards, section leader Sgt. Czerwinski tells me that the river company has just come off months of hard patrolling and fighting in the Falluja and Ramadi areas. This new assignment at Haditha Dam should be—

—A GOOD BREAK FOR US.

The next day, his unit is ambushed after landing on the river bank to investigate some small arms fire. Lance Cpl. Parrello, who piloted the boat I'd ridden on the day before, is killed. Three others are wounded, including Capt. Kuniholm, my coffee-drinking roommate at the dam, who had jumped on one of the boats on the spur of the moment.

He and the others are medivac'd out.

Within hours, Capt. Kuniholm's 21 pairs of black socks, his four year old's drawings, and all his other items are packed up for shipment to his family in North Carolina.

He will not be coming back. His right arm has been severed below the elbow.

A short time later, I leave Haditha Dam on a convoy bound for the Al Asad air base.

The Marines I'm with keep "eyes" on the Iraqi cars that pull over to let us through.

ANY ONE OF THESE VEHICLES COULD BE LOADED WITH BOMBS.

SEE THAT VEHICLE? HE'S GOT HIS HOOD UP.

WATCH THAT FUCKER!

J. SACCO 2-05

And I catch a glimpse of a man with a moustache as we punch by.

WITHIN A MONTH OF MY LEAVING, THE MARINES OF 1/23 AND THEIR ATTACHED UNITS SUFFERED SEVEN MORE FATALITIES.

December 2004. On the Euphrates River, in Iraq's volatile Anbar province, on one of the top levels of the Haditha Dam, isolated from the reserve marines of the 1st Battalion of the 23rd Regiment, which is headquartered here, two U.S.

servicemen are tasked with shaping a motley group from the Iraqi National Guard (I.N.G.) into the sort of self-motivated, competent soldiers that can—in the words of President George W. Bush—"stand up" so that "we can stand down."

DOWN! UP!

by Joe Sacco © 2006

And if anyone is going to help Iraqis save Iraq, it is Sgt. Tim Weaver, but they won't be saving anything, he'll tell you, until they get small unit formations into their skulls.

Unfortunately, this afternoon's quiz confirms that this lot can't tell its "skirmish left" from its "echelon right."

And that makes Sgt. Weaver one disgusted fifth-generation marine.

EVERYONE THAT MISSED ONE—

STAND UP!

Sgt. Weaver's prescription for one wrong answer is ten push ups.

DOWN! UP! DOWN! UP!

YOU JUST DID TEN FUCKING PUSH UPS AND YOU DIDN'T HAVE TO.

ALL RIGHT, WHO MISSED TWO?

YOU'RE DOING 20!

J. SACCO 8.06

84

J. SACCO 7.06

FOR THOSE OF YOU WHO ACED THE TEST, EX- CELLENT JOB!

YOU HAVE TO PAY ATTENTION BE- CAUSE IF YOUR FIRE TEAM LEADER GETS KILLED IN COMBAT, YOU'RE GOING TO HAVE TO STEP UP AND TAKE OVER.

NEXT WEEK WE GET ON THE RIFLE RANGE.

YOU'VE GOT TO KNOW WHAT YOU'RE DOING OR SOLDIERS ARE GOING TO GET SHOT IN THE BACK.

While the men go over the answers to the quiz, Sgt. Weaver steps over to where I've been sitting taking notes.

SOME OF THEM ARE UNEDU- CATED.

In fact, only five of the 14 can read and write.

THEY'RE BACK- WOODS BOYS.

SOME OF THEM HAVE NO COMMON SENSE, NO COMPREHEN- SION SKILLS.

It's time to check the make-up test of the guardsman who cheated.

Oops!

He still got three wrong!

I TOLD YOU WE COULD DO IT THE EASY WAY AND LEARN, OR WE CAN DO IT THROUGH PAIN!

Sgt. Weaver orders the fellow into a stress position and tells him to hold it for ten minutes.

EVERY TIME YOU STAND OR TOUCH YOUR LEGS OR ANY- THING, WE'LL START THE TEN MIN- UTES A- GAIN!

I'LL GET IN YOUR MIND!

Before too long, the guardsman squirms upright and drops his arms. He's made to start again. Minutes later he's babbling.

IF YOU WANT TO GO HOME TO MOMMA, I'LL CALL HER!

J. SACCO 7.06

85

Now it's Doc Saba's turn.

DON'T EVER WRITE ANSWERS ON YOUR HAND.

EVER.

THAT'S CHEATING.

CHEATING DISHONORS YOURSELF.

WHEN I SEE SGT. WEAVER, I FORGET EVERYTHING...

YOU NEED TO REMEMBER YOUR 'RIGHT' FROM YOUR 'LEFT.'

Sgt. Weaver, too, worries that they haven't got the basics down. He reviews hand signals they should know by now.

DIRECTION LEFT!

STOP FIRE!

ENEMY, 300 METERS!

They yell out the answers in English like happy school kids.

Sgt. Weaver promises <u>real</u> combat training after chow.

SO ALL OF YOU WHO ARE PISSED OFF AT ME, YOU CAN KICK MY ASS...

The Iraqis are given Meals Ready to Eat.

They pester Ahmed to translate what the packets and pouches contain.

THESE GUYS ARE IN MORE DANGER THAN WE ARE.

THERE'S MORE OF THEM GETTING KILLED OFF EVERY WEEK THAN AMERICANS AND COALITION FORCES.

WE GET THEM OUT OF THEIR ENVIRONMENT AND UP HERE 'CAUSE THERE'S NO TRIBAL CONNECTION AND THEY'LL BE ABLE TO FIGHT.

J. SACCO 7-06

In fact, none of these men, who were already in the I.N.G., knew they were in for this Marine boot camp stuff. One day they were locked in a room, and the next they were in vehicles heading for Haditha Dam. For security reasons they were not told where they were going; their loved ones still do not know they are here.

The idea is eventually to reunite them with their families at some location far from their home villages, thus snapping their old loyalties.

After their three-week course, Doc Saba tells me, they'll have a graduation ceremony where awards will be given to the best and the most-improved trainee.

WE'RE GETTING A PATCH DESIGNED FOR THEM, SOMETHING TO BE PROUD OF.

WITHOUT THAT PATCH, AS FAR AS WE'RE CONCERNED, YOU'RE NOT AN I.N.G. SOLDIER.

Doc Saba, who was attached to the scout snipers, and Sgt. Weaver, who was pulled from the battalion's motor transport unit, put this program together in just two weeks.

I LOVE DOING THIS SHIT.

I LOVE YELLING AT PEOPLE.

After lunch, Sgt. Weaver demonstrates the "basic warrior stance."

STEP! PLACÉ! STEP! PLACÉ!

It's time for the Iraqis to try.

BACK! BACK! BACK!

FORWARD! FORWARD! FORWARD!

J. SACCO 7·06

A few minutes later, the lesson disintegrates.

YOU'VE GOT SO MUCH ENERGY TO PLAY AROUND—?

EVERYONE, ON YOUR FACE!

DOWN! UP! DOWN! UP!

I DIDN'T TELL YOU TO STAND AROUND AND BOX AND KISS AND TOUCH EACH OTHER'S BUTTS!

PLAY TIME IS OVER!

THIS SHIT COULD SAVE YOUR LIFE!

Sgt. Weaver tries organizing them again, but pretty soon they're cruising for another round of push ups.

DOWN! UP!

YOU'RE FUCKING THE GROUND!

But Sgt. Weaver isn't satisfied he's made his point.

He gets them into a new position and makes them hold it till they collapse.

Doc Saba tells them he can be just as ferocious, but—

—I'M JUST NOT IN A SHOUTING MOOD TODAY...

IF SGT. WEAVER AND I CAN'T TRUST YOU WITH PAYING ATTENTION AND LISTENING TO US, THEN THERE'S NO WAY WE'RE GOING TO PUT A WEAPON IN YOUR HANDS.

J. SACCO 6.06

THIS IS NO JOKING MATTER. WE ARE TRAINING YOU FOR A REASON.

YOU JOINED ON YOUR OWN INTO THE I.N.G. I DIDN'T FORCE YOU TO JOIN.

BEING A SOLDIER IS NOT EASY WORK.

Meanwhile, one guy still hasn't come to his feet. He's complaining about his hips. Not even Sgt. Weaver can shout him off the ground.

Doc Saba listens to the guardsman, but Sgt. Weaver's not having any of it.

LOOK AT THAT GUY. HE SAYS HE'S 28 BUT HE LOOKS 40.

HE SIMPLY HAS NEVER EXERCISED IN HIS LIFE, THAT'S WHY HIS MUSCLES ARE ACHING.

WE HAVE TO TEAR DOWN THE RECRUITS IN ORDER TO BUILD THEM UP.

WE'RE NOT TRYING TO KILL YOU...

I AM.

The next morning, before sunrise, while the guardsmen are assembled on top of the dam to take showers in relays of four, I ask to speak to the trainee who has seemed the most serious about his instruction.

His name is Qaid;

he is 24;

and he speaks English.

Unlike most of the others, he is well schooled. He has a degree in mathematics from the educational college in Ramadi.

But teaching jobs are dependent on connections and corruption, he says, while—

—YOU CAN GO TO ANY I.N.G. CAMP...AND GET HIRED JUST LIKE THAT.

J. SACCO 8-06

And even though the I.N.G. is targeted relentlessly by the insurgents, it offers Qaid one of the only steady sources of income available to him.

I AM A POOR MAN.

THERE ARE 14 PEOPLE IN MY FAMILY...

IT'S A HARD SITUATION IN GENERAL.

Qaid has other reasons for earning money any way he can.

I WAS IN LOVE WITH A WOMAN, BUT I COULDN'T MARRY HER BECAUSE I AM VERY POOR AND SHE IS FROM A HIGH CLASS FAMILY. I'LL DO ANYTHING IN THE WORLD TO MARRY HER.

But now he is having second thoughts about the I.N.G.

I DIDN'T KNOW I WAS COMING TO HADITHA.

I DON'T WANT TO STAY IN THE GUARD.

FIRST THING, I LIKE THE CIVILIAN LIFE.

THE MILITARY LIFE NOW IN IRAQ IS UGLY.

THIRD, MOST OF THE OFFICERS ARE CORRUPT.

He says he intends to "quit" in a couple of months.

I HOPE IN THE FUTURE TO HAVE A SCHOLARSHIP TO GET TO ANY OTHER COUNTRY IN THE WORLD.

AND I WILL TRY TO GET ANOTHER CITIZENSHIP...

THEN I WILL BE HAPPY — BECAUSE I AM FINISHED WITH IRAQ.

RUN IN AND TELL OMER, IF HE CAN'T GET OUT OF THE SHOWER NOW, I'M GONNA CUT HIS DICK OFF!

I KNOW ARABIC, TOO:

'GET THE FUCK OVER HERE!'

THEY SEEM TO KNOW WHAT THAT MEANS.

J. SACCO 8·06

This morning, Sgt. Weaver is not in a pussyfooting mood.

YOU PUSH MY BUTTONS, I'M GOING TO FUCK YOU UP!

Even "good cop" Saba chimes in.

ANY OF YOU FUCK WITH MY SCHEDULE, I WILL RUN YOUR ASS TILL YOU PUKE, TILL YOU'RE CURLED UP LIKE A LITTLE BABY!

Today's class takes place on top of the dam. After some warm ups, the guardsmen are paired up to try the moves they learned yesterday. They seem enthusiastic about this kung fu stuff, about inflicting pain on their partners.

MAKE SURE YOU SPIN HIM!

DON'T FORCE HIM DOWN!

MAKE THAT RO-TATION!

NOW YOU'RE GO-ING TO DO IT FASTER!

DO NOT HURT EACH OTHER!

Sgt. Weaver demonstrates a counter-move to a behind-the-back bear hug, how to rap an assailant's knuckles un-til his hold is loosened.

OR YOU JUST HIT HIM IN THE FUCKIN' NUTS.

While the guardsmen continue their training, I ask Doc Saba to assess his raw material.

ONLY ABOUT HALF THESE RECRUITS ARE WORTH SOME-THING.

In any case, he says, this course is too short. They need six or even eight weeks' training to be "minimally" ready to patrol with marines.

J. SACCO 8.06

One of the younger trainees can't do a "leg sweep"...

so Sgt. Weaver does one for him.

Ouch!

MY HEAD! MY HEAD!

YOU'RE CRYING LIKE A FUCKING BABY!

YOU'RE A GROWN MAN, NOT A LITTLE BOY!

Doc Saba steps in. He thinks the fellow might actually be hurt.

MY HEAD!

HE'S PROBABLY NEVER BEEN IN A FIGHT IN HIS LIFE.

MY HEAD...

The kid sits out the rest of the lesson but he can't stop shaking.

By the way, everyone's shivering in the crisp December air.

ARE YOU ALL FUCKING COLD?

ON YOUR FACE!

DOWN! UP! DOWN! UP!

A few minutes later, Sgt. Weaver is at wit's end. Only two of the 14 guardsmen perform the hand-to-hand drill to his satisfaction.

ALL RIGHT, DOC. I'M DONE.

IT'S KILLING ME.

He thinks only five of the guardsmen are worth his time.

THE REST OF THEM, THEY ARE KIDS.

THEY ARE NOT MEN.

THE ONES THAT ARE MEN, THEY ARE RETARD-ED.

Today's lesson sputters to an end, and it's time for a pep talk.

WHEN THE FUCKIN' MUJ JUMPS IN YOUR FACE, YOU'LL START PISSING AND SHITTING YOUR PANTS!

INSTEAD OF BEING AN I.N.G. SOLDIER, YOU'LL GO HOME TO MOMMA AND PUT HER TITTIE IN YOUR MOUTH AND START SUCKING!

IF I WAS YOU, I'D TAKE THAT TITTIE OUT OF MY MOUTH...

GROW THE HELL UP...

AND GET THE JOB DONE!

Doc Saba lets them know about a group of Iraqi police just executed in Tikrit.

THE MUJ PULLED 12 POLICE OUT OF THEIR POLICE STATION... THEY'RE ALL DEAD.

AFTER THEY'D DONE KILLING THE POLICE OFFI-CERS, THEY THREW A SATCHEL CHARGE IN THE POLICE STA-TION AND BLEW IT UP.

THE MUJAHADEEN DON'T GIVE A SHIT ABOUT YOU.

WE'RE TRY-ING TO TEACH YOU THE TRAIN-ING SO YOU CAN STAY ALIVE.

THE MUJ ARE REAL.

THE BULLETS ARE REAL.

AND IF YOU GET KILLED, THAT'S REAL.

J. SACCO 7.06

He tells them they'll be expected to encourage others to join the I.N.G. Then:

PRESIDENT BUSH WANTS TO SEE YOUR COUNTRY SUCCEED.

PRESIDENT BUSH HAS HELPED YOUR COUNTRY A LOT...

DON'T LET HIM DOWN.

I DON'T THINK THEY GRASP WHY THEY'RE HERE.

After the session breaks up, I have a word with Ahmed, the translator, in the guardsmen's quarters. He has echoed Sgt. Weaver's commands all day, yell for yell.

He tells me about another translator, a friend of his, who recently was killed by insurgents.

THEY MUTILATED HIM AND LEFT HIM WITH HIS I.D. AND HIS PAYCHECK.

HE WAS WITH A MALE AND A FEMALE INTERPRETER, ALSO KILLED.

AFTER I HEARD ABOUT THEM, I WAS SHOCKED.

MY FAMILY IS PUTTING PRESSURE ON ME TO STOP THIS WORK.

BUT I'D WORK FOR FREE.

I WANT THESE PEOPLE TO GET ON THEIR FEET...

IF THEY DIE, THEY EACH BETTER KILL ONE OF THE INSURGENTS.

ALL THESE GUYS WANT TO QUIT.

THEY DON'T WANT TO DO THE HARD WORK.

THEY'RE ALL THINKING THAT THE AMERICANS GET PISSED OFF AND HAVE COME TO CHEW THEIR ASSES.

ARERICANS WANT THEM TO BE STRONG.

J. SACCO 8.06

I spend a little time with a few guardsmen who are willing to talk to me.

They all seem to come from big families.

Most were out of work or underemployed when they joined the I.N.G., which pays a few hundred dollars per month—good money here.

They say they are proud to be guardsmen...

that they want to fight the insurgents...

and that they think the training they're undergoing is good.

I wonder if they are telling me what they think I want to hear. I wonder if they think I am going to report what they say to Sgt. Weaver or Petty Officer Second Class Saba.

I search out Qaid, who seems to have few reservations about speaking his mind.

THESE MARTIAL ARTS ARE NOT EFFECTIVE BECAUSE YOU CAN'T RESIST THE MUJAHADEEN WITH YOUR HANDS.

THE MUJAHADEEN COME TO YOU ARMED, THEY'LL SURROUND YOU, TAKE YOU TO AN AREA WHERE THERE ARE NO PEOPLE, AND KILL YOU.

J. SACCO 7·06

TRAUMA ON LOAN

I. 'JUST CONFESS'

by Joe Sacco ©2006

98

According to the two men, American troops then entered the building "from all sides," including from the roof.

Sherzad: "They were yelling... and aiming their guns. And they started beating everybody."

Along with others in the building, they were cuffed, hooded, and driven away. It was nighttime when the vehicle stopped. "They kicked us off," according to Thahe.

"We fell on the ground... Our hands were still tied behind our backs, and we were still hooded."

Thahe's left shoulder was dislocated in the fall.

When their hoods were removed, they say they found themselves in one of Saddam Hussein's presidential palaces—standing in front of a cage of lions. The lions, evidently, once had been the personal property of Uday, one of Saddam's notorious sons.

One by one, the detainees were taken to the cage and, according to Sherzad, told to confess.

WHAT DO YOU WANT US TO CONFESS?

YOU DON'T KNOW WHY YOU'RE HERE? JUST CONFESS!

Thahe: "They opened the door... We went in, maybe a meter..."

"But when the lions came running toward us, they pulled us outside..."

"I lost consciousness. I was unconscious most of the time now. And the way they woke me up was by beating me..."

The men then were taken to a wall behind the cage.

THE OFFICER HAS DECIDED TO EXECUTE YOU BY SHOOTING. SO YOU BETTER CONFESS.

Sherzad: "And we didn't confess because we didn't know what they wanted us to say."

J. SACCO 12.05

YOU KNOW WHEN YOU WATCH MOVIES AND YOU HEAR THE WORD 'FIRE!'

IT WAS THE SAME.

THEY SAID, 'FIRE!' AND THEY FIRED.

"I fell down to the ground. And then I heard the soldiers' laughter. So I started looking at my body, trying to find a trace of blood. I realized it was just a mock execution..."

According to Thahe and Sherzad, by then a number of detainees had pissed on themselves.

They spent the night shackled to a tennis court fence, and the next day they were taken to the prison at Baghdad's international airport, where they were made to run a gauntlet of baton-wielding soldiers before reaching their cells.

II. 'THE LION THING'

In America, another sort of gauntlet awaited them:

Cameramen!

Photographers!

Reporters!

By the time I met them in Washington, D.C., their lawyers, who include members of the American Civil Liberties Union and Human Rights First, fretted that all the interviews had pushed their clients to the edge.

ATTORNEY HINA SHAMSI, HUMAN RIGHTS FIRST

SOMETIMES WE DON'T KNOW WHEN THEY'VE HAD ENOUGH, AND SOMETIMES THEY DON'T KNOW THEMSELVES UNTIL AFTERWARDS.

Thahe and Sherzad's visit to the States is meant to draw attention to their legal complaint, which alleges "torture or other cruel, inhuman or degrading punishment" while they were in U.S. military custody.

They "are representative of so many hundreds or thousands of others...whose shockingly brutal mistreatment" is ultimately Mr. Rumsfeld's responsibility, according to Emily Whitfield, the ACLU's media relations director.

In effect, Thahe and Sherzad are standing in for all the hooded and beaten. For this case, they are sacrificial detainees.*

* THEY ARE JOINED BY SIX OTHER PLAINTIFFS: FOUR AFGHANS AND TWO IRAQIS

J. SACCO 12-05

So when their lawyers expressed misgivings about Thahe and Sherzad reopening their wounds for one last journalist—me!—when they hinted *my* interview might be cancelled, I wanted to snap back—

"Come on!"

"You brought them here to reopen their wounds."

"No point worrying about their feelings *now*."

Besides, the media blitz has had an impact. Even the chief defendant has taken notice.

THE LION THING WAS MENTIONED AT THE RUMSFELD BRIEFING.

Yes, it's "the lion thing" that is raising eyebrows. Much else of what Thahe and Sherzad allege — the shackling in extreme temperatures, the electric shocks, the desecration of the Koran — might seem ho-hum to an American public that has long digested the enormities of Abu Ghraib.

And at his press conference, Mr. Rumsfeld called Thahe and Sherzad's lion story "farfetched" and referred to Al-Qaeda documents that—

— TRAIN PEOPLE, TERRORISTS, TO LIE ABOUT THEIR TREATMENT.

Thahe and Sherzad might take exception to Mr. Rumsfeld's implication that they have studied Al-Qaeda manuals or that they are "terrorists."

Neither of them was ever charged with anything by the Americans.

III. "WHAT IS YOUR FAVORITE SPORT?" WHEN I WAS FIRST TAKEN FOR INTERROGATION, I WAS HAPPY.

I THOUGHT, NOW I CAN EXPLAIN MYSELF.

"But the first question was—

WHERE IS SADDAM?*

"I laughed, and he hit me."

After perfunctory questions about weapons of mass destruction, Al-Qaeda, etc., the interrogator asked—

WHAT IS YOUR FAVORITE BREAKFAST?

WHAT IS YOUR FAVORITE SPORT?

WHAT TIME DO YOU GO TO SLEEP?

WHY WAS HE ASKING YOU THOSE LAST THINGS?

I DON'T KNOW.

But then, does Sherzad know why he was subjected to "simulat[ed] anal rape" with a water bottle? Does Thahe know why "one or more soldiers in the presence of male and female soldiers inserted their fingers" into his anus?

* SADDAM HUSSEIN WAS STILL IN HIDING WHEN THIS INTERROGATION TOOK PLACE

J. SACCO 12-05

I've quoted Thahe's and Sherzad's sexual assault allegations from the lawsuit. Their attorneys ask me not to bring up the subject with the men. When CNN broke that ground rule and badgered Thahe about his ordeal, he was retraumatized, I'm told.

IV. 'I HAVE NO DESIRE TO TELL A SAD STORY'

In the morning, an interview with 'Time' magazine; in the afternoon, a meeting with earnest Senate staffers who promise to relay Thahe and Sherzad's story to their bosses.

And now one of the attorneys suggests a quick get-together with her colleagues in an office nearby.

IT'S UP TO YOU.

But Thahe is only being diplomatic. He boards the van rented for the day's activities and waits for his handlers to follow.

WE WANT TO GO SEE THE WHITE HOUSE.

The lawyers are sensitive to the moods of their clients. The rest of the day will be given over to sight-seeing.

For an hour or two, Thahe and Sherzad smile in front of America's monuments to liberty.

But the cell phones are ringing again. A senator has agreed to meet with Thahe and Sherzad personally.

When? Now!

Thahe is almost despondent. He has to remind himself why he's here.

WE DIDN'T COME AS TOURISTS.

Sherzad, on the other hand, won't have it.

AFTER SEEING THIS BEAUTIFUL VIEW, I HAVE NO DESIRE TO TELL A SAD STORY.

The attorneys turn down the senator. And they tell Thahe and Sherzad they will get to see the White House in the morning.

V. THE AIRPORT

AT THE AIRPORT, THERE WERE 75 TO 150 DETAINEES IN EACH TENT.

"There was a place for people to sit, but not to sleep. The ground was earth. We were given one blanket. My pillow was my shoes."

"I had a beard. I had long hair just like a beast."

J. SACCO 12-05

102

"Each tent had its own guard... The guard would bring a folding chair... and he'd sit with his water, and he had a carton of cigarettes, and he smoked as much as he wanted.

"We were allowed two cigarettes a day.

"One time, a very ugly person came.

I'M NOT GOING TO GIVE YOU YOUR CIGARETTES.

I'M GOING TO THROW A CIGARETTE, AND IF YOU CATCH IT IN YOUR MOUTH YOU CAN HAVE IT.

IF IT FALLS ON THE GROUND, YOU DON'T GET IT.

"The soldiers saw this funny situation, and they were coming over.

"One of the detainees was in front, and his actions were like a dog's.

"The soldier was faking as if he would throw the cigarette this way or that way.

"The soldiers were laughing. They gave him a lot of cigarettes...

"It was my turn. I told him in very basic English:

I WANT TWO CIGA-RETTES ONLY, PLEASE.

I DON'T WANT TO DO THAT.

"He opened the wire and came in... He beat me and he cursed me."

VI. THE WHITE HOUSE

There's a train to catch back to New York, but a promise is a promise, and in the morning Thahe and Sherzad are taken to see the White House.

And there they find a lone protester in a painfully familiar pose.

BAN ALL TORTURE NOW

J. SACCO 12-05

VIII. RELEASE

Honestly, I've been gentle.

I haven't pushed.

I've jumped over whole allegations, entire beatings and humiliations.

I've curbed my enthusiasm for detail.

Yet even without the hints from the attorney monitoring our conversation, it's clear to me that Thahe has had enough.

CONTINUE WITH ME BECAUSE I'M STRONGER THAN HE IS.

So I go on with Sherzad for a few minutes more, but I know it's time to leave.

Because after awhile, in certain situations, a journalist in a room begins to smell; even *he* notices.

Still— I have one more question. Just one more and I'm going.

How were you re-leased?

YOU KNOW, THE RELEASE IS RANDOM, JUST LIKE THE ARREST.

"Once you're released, you don't believe it. You look behind you because you're so scared that they're going to jump you and arrest you again.

"And I did not believe that I was released until I arrived at my house and saw my children.

"And I closed the door.

"And I asked my brother to bring me a lock so I could lock the door from the inside.

"And they were laughing at me."

I pack my pen and notebook and tape recorder.

I get up to go.

I tell Thahe and Sherzad that I was honored to meet them.

I thank them.

I wish them a good journey back to Iraq.

And, once again, they are released.

J. SACCO 12-05

105

Iraq, Notes

I've heard much criticism of embedded journalism, including by people whose opinions I respect, and though I was personally opposed to the invasion of Iraq, I thought it would be worth my while to see things from the standpoint of those at the tip of the spear of the American imperial project. Of course a journalist begins to see things from the perspective of a marine when one is on patrol with marines, but to me that is the point. Ultimately combat troops are narrowly focused on the matter at hand, and generally they are more interested in taking care of each other than accomplishing anything more patriotic sounding. In that respect, almost all combat stories are the same, and I imagine "Complacency Kills" could just as well have been set during the wars in Vietnam or Korea. From that perspective, I don't think my story added anything new to the immense literature of "men at war," but what journalist doesn't want to see everything firsthand? The *Guardian* staff provided me with generous logistical support and didn't interfere editorially at all; the marines treated me with respect and kindness. I thank them all.

"Down! Up!" is a better story because it gets to the heart of the above-mentioned imperial project: the disconnect between what the results-oriented American overseers want and what the bewildered and traumatized locals are able or willing to do. Aside from a translator or two, the national guardsmen were the only Iraqis I spoke to while I was in the country. To me, they were civilians who needed a livelihood who had put on a uniform; I felt deeply sorry for them. I wrote the story as it played out in front of me. I was wary of working again for *Harper's*, but Roger Hodge, the new editor, made my second experience with the magazine a positive one.

Reporting for "Trauma on Loan," the story of Thahe Sabbar and Sherzad Khalid, was a very frustrating experience.

I spent two or three days traveling with them to let them get comfortable with me before our formal interview. Consequently, when one of them told me he was going to tell me something he hadn't told other journalists, I thought I'd earned his confidence. The human rights attorney present immediately stopped him. She obviously had his interests in mind, but I resented the interference. Even when advocates and journalists share the same values they might not necessarily have the same goals. A journalist wants to know everything and insists on his own discrimination whether and how to present loaded material.

"Complacency Kills" appeared in the *Guardian Weekend*, February 26, 2005.

"Down! Up!" appeared in *Harper's Magazine*, April 2007.

"Trauma on Loan" appeared in the *Guardian Weekend*, January 21, 2006.

MIGRATION

Globalization!

Italian and French vessels snag bluefins in huge nets and then transfer them to Maltese fish farmers who keep the tuna captive until the day they're harvested, packed, and flown—still fresh—to Japan.

And so what begins in the Mediterranean Sea ends with happy burps in Tokyo's restaurants.

THE UNWANTED

by Joe Sacco ©2009

But here, off the coast of Malta, the fishermen harpooning and gutting the day's quota bristle at the mention of a darker feather in globalization's cap, the 12,500 mostly Sub-Saharan Africans desperate to reach Europe who have washed up on the island's shore.*

The fishermen want to know what Malta has got to do with Africans.

I SAY IF THEY'RE SOMALI, THEY SHOULD GO TO ITALY.

Italy once owned Somalia, James reasons.

AND BELGIUM SHOULD TAKE THE ONES FROM THE IVORY COAST.

THE BELGIANS WERE THE ONES WHO WERE THERE.

*AS OF AUG. 2009

Actually, it was the French, but I don't have time to correct James before he's bounded across the deck to decapitate another tuna.

J. SACCO B-09

109

And the Maltese don't particularly want them to reach Malta either.

In one notorious incident, African migrants held on to a tuna net for two days after their boat sank while the Maltese fishermen towing the net refused to take them onboard.

Nor would they take them ashore.

The owner of the Maltese vessel didn't want to delay bringing in his catch.

It was left to the Italian navy to rescue the migrants.

But the Maltese cannot always avoid the issue, and they have become the unhappy hosts of many of those rescued at sea or desperate, after losing their way, for any shore.

IT'S NOT THAT THE MALTESE DON'T WANT TO HELP.

BUT WE'RE TOO SMALL FOR THE NUMBER WE HAVE.

WHERE ARE THEY GOING TO STAY?

IMAGINE IF THEY KEEP COMING.

The Maltese archipelago is indeed tiny, a total of 122 square miles...

and with 400,000 residents it is one of the world's most densely populated places.

0 2 4 6 8 10
MILES

MALTA

ST. PAUL'S BAY
SLIEMA
ST. ANTON GARDENS
VALLETTA
MARSA
TA'KANDJA
SAFI
BIRZEBBUGA
HAL FAR

ONLY SITES MENTIONED IN THIS STORY ARE LABELED

In 2001, looking ahead to a potential influx of what are now termed "irregular immigrants," Malta opened a facility to hold 80 people.

The next year 1,600 Africans landed.

The numbers kept rising.

There is a story going around that has gained traction in Malta. I heard it four times.

An African tells a Maltese policeman, "Keep the boats because one day you'll be on them."

THE MAYOR

Time for me to come clean:

I was born in Malta.

My family immigrated to Australia when I was a baby...

and the Australian government, eager to populate its large continent with white-faced Europeans, paid most of our passage.

But no one sent the Africans—the vast majority of whom are single Muslim men—an invitation to Malta, a Catholic and, until recently, homogeneous country.

When African immigrants arrive here, they are welcomed by detention for up to a year and a half (we'll get to that later) before being released to open centers, where they can come and go as they please.

Some of these facilities are in the heart of Maltese communities.

One of the largest is in a disused trade school in Marsa, a working-class town of 6,000.

J. SACCO 9·09

Debono takes me to Prince Albert Street, where a row of houses is sandwiched between the open center and Marsa's industrial zone.

We pull over to speak to some people sitting on their stoop.

When Debono explains in Maltese that I've come from America to find out what the locals think of the African immigrants, one woman named Rita asks him,

WHAT SHOULD WE SAY?

THAT WE'RE FOR THEM OR AGAINST THEM?

She laughs when she realizes I understand the language, but then she gets right to it...

YESTERDAY ONE OF THEM — ABOUT 12 A.M., WHEN MY 11-YEAR-OLD NEPHEW WAS SITTING ON THE SOFA PLAYING WITH THE COMPUTER — ONE OF THEM OPENED THE DOOR AND WALKED IN.

Her sister chased off the man, Rita says.

Victor has a message for the immigrants.

AT LEAST TURN YOUR BACK WHEN YOU PEE.

Manuel drives a bus, and so many blacks use it, he says, that the Maltese won't get on board.

He says one bus driver was beaten by Africans when he told them the bus was already full up.

IT'S LIKE YOU'RE SPEAKING TO AN ANIMAL.

EVEN AN ANIMAL UNDERSTANDS "FULL UP."

Debono explains that Marsa is a community where "everyone trusts each other," and it has become unnerved by the great number of constantly "changing faces" in the open center. But crime hasn't increased, he says, so he tries to calm the fears of his constituents.

He himself is reconciled to the presence of the open center in Marsa, if not its size.

[THE MALTESE] HAVE TO UNDERSTAND THAT YOU CAN'T SAY MALTA IS ONLY FOR THE MALTESE.

So will Malta ever go back to the way it was?

NO, IT WILL NEVER GO BACK.

Later, over a drink in Valletta, the capital city, he further ponders Malta's unwanted guests.

EVEN IF YOU ARE AGAINST THEM, YOU HAVE TO LIVE WITH THEM, AND IT'S SOMETHING HORRIBLE TO LIVE WITH SOMEONE YOU DON'T LIKE.

IT IS DANGEROUS.

In fact, Lowell's wider world view, which blames the Jews for most of the world's ills (including the African migrations), holds up Hitler as "The Hero," and envisions a Latin-speaking, all-white empire (Imperium Europa), is generally unknown to the Maltese, few of whom have read his incendiary books.

IMPERIUM EUROPA LOGO

CREDO
JPS

SUBTITLED: "A BOOK FOR THE VERY FEW"

IMPERIVM EVROPA

SUBTITLED: "THE BOOK THAT CHANGED THE WORLD."

Lowell received 4,500 Maltese votes in the 2009 European Parliament elections, triple his tally in a previous contest.

That would be a significant number in a Maltese general election, which are often decided by a few thousand votes.

Though many dismiss Lowell's showing as a protest vote, his and other right wing voices have induced many mainstream politicians to assert their own anti-immigrant credentials. The African arrivals are now Malta's number one political issue.

At a cafe near St. Anton Gardens, on a scorchingly hot day that saw the landing of 44 more Africans on Malta, Lowell describes the rise of his Imperium Europa movement.

AT FIRST WE...WERE DENIGRATED, LAUGHED AT, IGNORED, TREATED VERY BADLY BY THE MEDIA. BUT EVENTUALLY WE MANAGED TO RAISE A CONSCIOUSNESS IN THE PEOPLE...

EVERY BOATLOAD LIKE THE ONE THAT LANDED THIS MORNING IS AN ALARM BELL TO THE PEOPLE.

J. SACCO 9-09

118

J. SACCO 9-09

But someone has taken the extreme right's message to heart.

Arsonists have targeted the homes or property of those considered sympathetic to the immigrants, including journalists, Jesuits, and a lawyer.

Our interview concluded, Lowell and I walk through the gardens, where he spots a black man with three children.

DO YOU SEE?

THEY ARE BREEDING FURIOUSLY IN OUR MIDST.

IT'S THE SUPPLANTING OF OUR POPULATION BY AN INVADING, ALIEN ONE...

BREEDING FURIOUSLY!

THEY CUSS YOU IN THEIR LANGUAGE WHEN YOU PASS. MOST OF THE WOMEN THEY COVER THEIR NOSE.

CLEMENT

MALTESE PEOPLE ARE RACIST... THE MALTESE BELIEVE IF YOU'RE AN AFRICAN IMMIGRANT, YOU ARE NOT SCHOOLED AT ALL. THEY LOOK DOWN ON YOU.

TEMITOPE

I BELIEVE IF THERE WOULD BE MORE IMMIGRANTS THEY WOULD STOP [THEIR ABUSE]. BECAUSE IF WE HAVE MORE NUMBERS, WE WILL TAKE ACTIONS.

YOUSEF

THERE IS NO CONNECTION BETWEEN MALTESE AND AFRICANS. IF YOU MEET THEM, SOME RESPECT YOU. MOST, THEY INSULT YOU.

ABDULLAH

J. SACCO 9.09

THE ERITREAN

He will not give me his name.

He says his family would be at risk if his identity were revealed.

I tell him to make up a name for me, anything, "John," if he likes.

OKAY.

"JOHN."

John would certainly be in danger back in his homeland. In 2002 Malta forcibly returned more than 220 Eritreans; they were immediately imprisoned on their arrival. Many were tortured, and some died from their mistreatment.

John's long, hard journey to Malta began in 2001 when he and thousands of other University of Asmara students refused an Eritrean government order to work the whole summer without pay.

More than 2,000 students, including John, were arrested and loaded onto trucks.

J. SACCO 9·09

He had been on track for a university job, which normally would have counted as national service. Instead he was next ordered into the army even though he had already fulfilled his military obligation. His transfer requests were turned down.

Three years went by.

"I was assigned to a place where I could do nothing... I had no job... I was in the military because it was a punishment."

Finally, he publically confronted an officer about his situation.

I'M NOT ASKING TO WORK FOR MONEY...

I NEED TO BE ASSIGNED TO A PLACE WHERE I CAN CONTRIBUTE.

"I [knew] that it is risky to speak in a meeting in Eritrea because there is no freedom of expression at all."

He was arrested and jailed the same day.

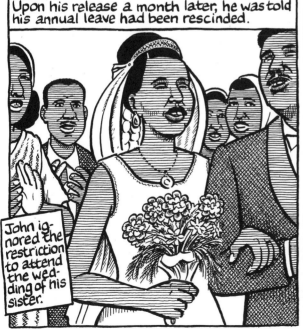

Upon his release a month later, he was told his annual leave had been rescinded.

John ignored the restriction to attend the wedding of his sister.

The military police were now looking for him. He decided to flee the country.

J. SACCO 10·09

123

He spent the equivalent of about 100 Euros* to illegally obtain the permission slip necessary to travel between towns in Eritrea.

He boarded a bus for a village on the Sudanese border, which took him through 22 checkpoints.

* 100 EUROS WERE APPROX. $125 THEN

The closer he got to the frontier, the more frequent the checkpoints became, he says.

"You have to state on the piece of paper from which division of the army you are [from]...So they can simply call and check, if they want."

But in John's case, no one bothered to.

"It's a matter of luck," he says.

For about 800 Euros, a smuggler guided him across the Sudanese border.

"There are guards everywhere... If they catch you while crossing the border...they shoot you. So there is no compromise.

"You have to run...

"I left at 7 o'clock in the evening, and it took me the whole night..."

He turned himself in to the Sudanese police, who released him three days later to the desolate U.N. refugee camp in Kassala.

Almost nothing was provided, he says, and Eritrean forces were known to raid the camp to drag refugees back across the border.

J. SACCO 10-09

124.

He decided to leave Kassala for the Sudanese capital, Khartoum, with a one-week pass.

"You [are] not allowed to simply leave and stay in Khartoum. You pay some money and you hand in your [U.N.] ID card to the police, just to make sure you will come back."

But John knew he would not be returning to Kassala for his ID.

Once in Khartoum "if [the police] arrested you for some reason, if you didn't have a residence card, there [was] a risk of deportation...

"Without having legal status you don't feel safe to simply live.

"You feel that everyone is looking at you...

"If you see the police ...you go far [to] the other side."

He stayed with an Eritrean friend, but John couldn't speak Arabic or find a job.

"I could not see any future."

His family sent him money to reach Europe.

THEY KNEW THAT THE SAHARA DESERT AND THE MEDITERRANEAN ARE RISKY. I MIGHT DIE ON THE WAY.

BUT... IF I WAS DEPORTED BACK TO ERITREA, THEY KNEW WHAT WOULD HAPPEN TO ME...

J. SACCO 10·09

He paid Eritrean contacts $200 to pass him along to Sudanese smugglers, who had gathered a group of would-be migrants—Eritreans, Ethiopians, Somalis, and Sudanese.

HOW DID YOU TRAVEL?

THERE WERE THREE CARS. WE WERE...MORE THAN 100 PEOPLE.

100 PEOPLE IN THREE CARS? HOW IS IT POSSIBLE?

IT IS DIFFICULT FOR SOMEONE TO BELIEVE THIS.

He found himself hanging onto the roof of a Land Cruiser.

"You simply have nothing to do."

"You simply push one another."

"You simply go like that."

After traveling three days and nights they were handed over to Libyan smugglers in the middle of the desert.

Each of the migrants had to pay another $300.

J. SACCO 10·09

126

The Libyans drove them to an oasis and then suddenly abandoned them to pick up another lot of migrants.

"They wanted more money to bring other people. Because other smugglers [would] take them if they didn't."

The next day, Sudanese resistance fighters showed up and robbed the stranded group. Most of the migrants had prepared a wad of money for just such an eventuality.

"Some of us gave $50, $10..."

"I paid $30."

After 12 days, when they were almost out of food, the Libyans returned with 100 additional migrants.

"We were ready to fight the Libyans," says John.

WE DON'T TRUST YOU ANYMORE.

The Libyans agreed to take the first group onward, and two days later passed them off to another band of smugglers, who charged each person an additional $50.

"It was the Sahara desert. We didn't want to stay even for one [more] hour in the desert. So we gave [the] money."

In a village outside of Benghazi, John was parceled off with about 20 others to a middleman "who bought us, like a commodity" and who would now sell his trafficked guests to another set of smugglers, but not before charging the migrants $200 each himself.

AND THOSE OF YOU WHO DON'T PAY, I'LL KICK YOU OUT OF MY HOME.

The new smugglers were Ethiopians, who—for an additional $200 each—drove them the 1,000 kilometers to Tripoli in a hidden compartment inside a tomato truck.

They were packed so tightly that they had been compelled to leave behind all their belongings.

"And if you hear the [truck] stopping, you have to keep quiet...because it might be stopping at a checkpoint."

J. SACCO 10·09

128

At last they reached Tripoli, but "Tripoli was the most horrible place I saw on my journey. It was very hostile. The police, the people. Very, very, very hostile towards immigrants.

"The people, especially children, stop you in the street and threaten you with a knife and ask you for money."

Adults never intervened to stop the young thieves, he says. "Nobody cared."

He was staying with 200 other migrants in a building owned by an Ethiopian trafficker.

"The police might come at any time.

"The Libyans ...knew that a lot of black people lived in this place.

"A lot of children [came] when they need[ed] money."

John decided he would be safer elsewhere. He moved to the outskirts of the city.

Two days later the building he'd left was raided by the police and its occupants were hauled away to the notorious detention camp at Kufra, John says.

He lay low for months and then paid $1,000 to an Eritrean who put him in contact with Libyans who could facilitate a Mediterranean crossing.

J. SACCO 10-09

The Libyans took him into a hiding place which began filling up with Africans hoping to make the same voyage. The 25 days there were tense, he says, with their hosts sometimes threatening to throw them all into the street.

It was now July 2006.

On the appointed day, before sunrise, the traffickers put 50 of the Africans onto a boat and sent them on their way to Europe.

They were caught by a Libyan patrol.

John had a space on the second boat due to leave that morning.

Despite the fate of the first vessel, he and the others pressed the Libyans to let them attempt the crossing.

WHAT WE WANTED AT THIS TIME WAS—A CHANCE!

TO BE ON THE SEA AND ON A BOAT...

THEN IT IS OUR LUCK IF SOMETHING HAPPENED, IF WE DROWNED OR THE POLICE CAME.

BUT THEY HAVE TO DO THEIR JOB: TAKE US TO THE SEA AND PROVIDE A BOAT.

The Libyans assigned a captain from among the migrants and then turned on the motor for them.

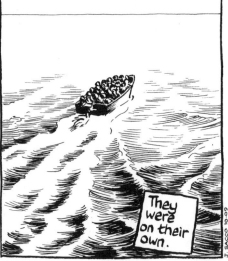

They were on their own.

DETENTION

Once they land in Malta, all "irregular immigrants" are locked up and guarded in closed detention centers. Only those considered vulnerable — minors and pregnant women, for example — are fast-tracked out.

John, the Eritrean who arrived in Malta in 2006, remembers,

NOBODY TELLS YOU ABOUT YOUR OBLIGATIONS OR YOUR RIGHTS... NOBODY EXPLAINS WHAT IS GOING TO HAPPEN.

IT IS REALLY STRESSFUL [FOR] DETAINEES AND CREATES A SYSTEM OF FRUSTRATION... YOU LOSE HOPE.

"[We] are people who are in need of help.

"On the contrary, they create a feeling that we are criminals and we need to be guarded by soldiers.

"[The detention centers] should be [staffed by] civilians and those who know how to take care of asylum seekers, who are victims of persecution and rape and all these things..."

J. SACCO 11.09

133

Carmelo Mifsud Bonnici, Minister of Justice and Home Affairs, who is most responsible for policy regarding immigrants, tells me,

THE DETENTION POLICY IS ODIOUS FOR US... BUT IT IS A NECESSITY.

He says the immigrants are an "unknown factor," that for "security reasons" they have to be screened to determine their backgrounds as "the majority do not have identification."

I CANNOT [ALLOW]... PERSONS RUNNING AROUND OUR STREETS WITH NO ACCOMMODATION...

KNOCKING ON DOORS TO GET FOOD,

WITHOUT ANY IDEA WHERE THEY CAME FROM,

AND WITH THE BIG IDEA THAT EUROPE IS AN EL DORADO.

Because deep in the government's heart is the suspicion that many if not most arrivals are economic migrants and not, as almost 100 percent of them claim, victims of war or persecution and that they often falsify their stories to wrangle some form of humanitarian protection— and legal status— from their reluctant hosts.

Refugee Commissioner Mario Friggieri, who runs the busy office that receives and decides on applications for asylum, tells me,

IT IS EASY TO SAY, 'I WAS IN MY COUNTRY AND I WAS PERSECUTED FOR MY POLITICAL OPINION...'

ANYBODY CAN SAY THAT.

YOU HAVE TO PROVE IT.

J. SACCO 11·09

Malta now separates detainees who are most likely to be rejected —West Africans—from those who stand a good chance—East Africans. When the hopefuls and the hopeless intermingled, the former sometimes lauded it over the latter, I'm told, which led to fighting between nationalities.

The Maltese government turns down my request to visit the detention center at Safi, which is "dedicated to rejected asylum seekers."

Lt. Col. Brian Gatt, who heads the Detention Service, the joint force of police and army personnel who guard the detainees, tells me,

THE PROBLEM WITH SAFI IS THAT IF THEY SEE A JOURNALIST, THEY GO BERSERK.

THEY COME OUT WITH POSTERS. THEY MAKE A LOT OF NOISE.

THE TENSION RISES VERY QUICKLY.

In fact, the model facility I'm allowed to visit, Ta' Kandja, had its own riot just three weeks earlier.

"There were 315 Somalis trying to break out," Gatt says. The guards were unarmed, he adds, "so obviously we came to blows."

The Somalis were demanding immediate release.

(Those granted some form of humanitarian protection are generally released within about six months. Those turned down may remain detained for a maximum of a year and a half.)

J. SACCO 11·09

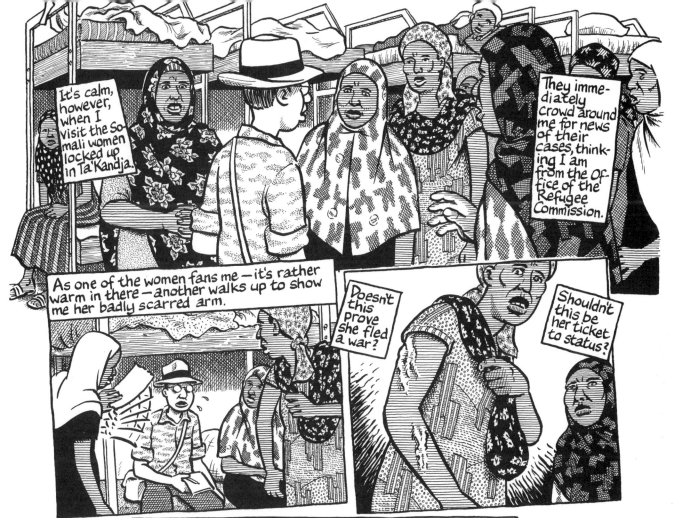

It's calm, however, when I visit the Somali women locked up in Ta'Kandja.

They immediately crowd around me for news of their cases, thinking I am from the Office of the Refugee Commission.

As one of the women fans me — it's rather warm in there — another walks up to show me her badly scarred arm.

Doesn't this prove she fled a war?

Shouldn't this be her ticket to status?

Because not even the Somalis can count on protection. In this room, 20 of 44 women have already had their asylum applications rejected.

Raha, who says she has spent 13 months in detention, is appealing her rejection to the Refugee Appeals Board.

I APPEAL, APPEAL, APPEAL, BUT I DIDN'T GET ANY RESULT.

I don't tell her that of the thousands of asylum seekers in Malta who have appealed their rejections, "less than ten" have seen their decisions overturned, according to Refugee Commissioner Friggieri.

As I leave the women, they rush to the door, forgetting me and eyeing Michael Cassar, the officer who runs the compound.

NEXT WEEK, NEXT WEEK, I'M GOING TO GET FREE?

But he has nothing to tell her. That's not his department.

J. SACCO 12-09

137

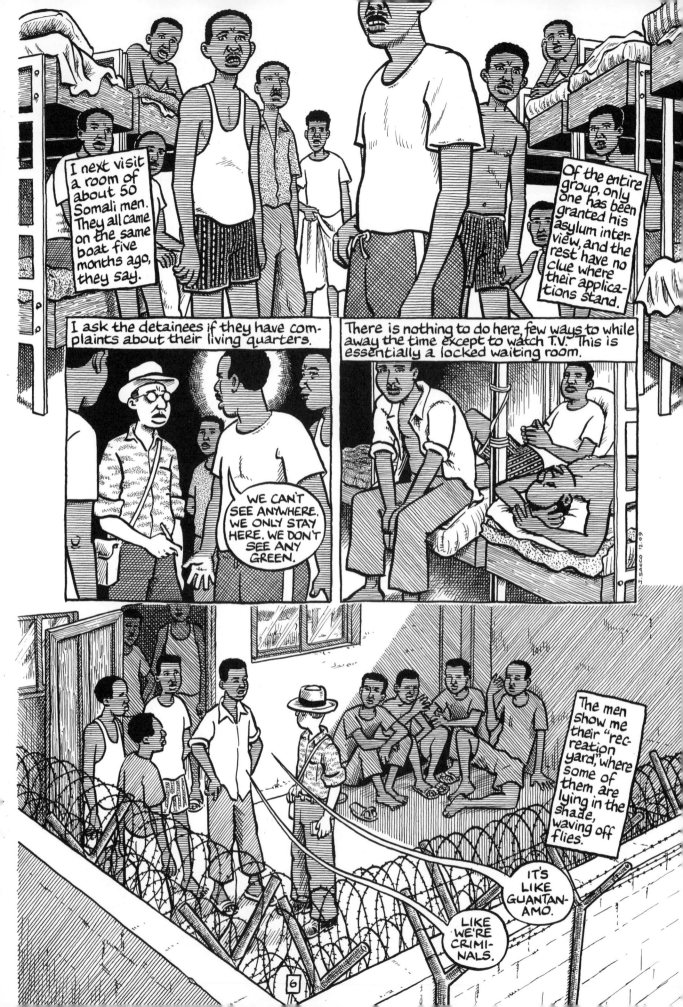

I next visit a room of about 50 Somali men. They all came on the same boat five months ago, they say.

Of the entire group, only one has been granted his asylum interview, and the rest have no clue where their applications stand.

I ask the detainees if they have complaints about their living quarters.

WE CAN'T SEE ANYWHERE. WE ONLY STAY HERE. WE DON'T SEE ANY GREEN.

There is nothing to do here, few ways to while away the time except to watch T.V. This is essentially a locked waiting room.

The men show me their "recreation yard," where some of them are lying in the shade, waving off flies.

IT'S LIKE GUANTANAMO.

LIKE WE'RE CRIMINALS.

I won't vouch for Ta'Kandja resembling Guantanamo, but several human rights reports have blasted Malta's detention facilities:

"unacceptable from the point of view of human dignity";

"migrants...are not treated as well as incarcerated criminals";

"unacceptable for a civilized country and untenable in Europe";

"disastrous sanitary facilities";

"clearly inhuman and degrading."

Like all Maltese officials I meet, Lt. Col. Gatt scoffs at most criticism of the nation's detention policy and facilities.

AS A GENERAL RULE, THE PEOPLE IN DETENTION ARE TREATED WITH HUMANITY.

He denies they suffer mental health problems due to their prolonged detention.

As to the charges of degraded facilities, Gatt says, "West Africans take pride in keeping their areas clean [but] East Africans don't give a damn ... The majority are Muslim, they are Arab-oriented, and living in squalor...for them is no problem."

In any case, Gatt tells me, Malta has limited resources, and when the immigrants started landing in numbers, "we didn't have any purpose-built structures to accommodate [them]."

Father Joseph Cassar, director of Jesuit Refugee Service, which does advocacy work on behalf of detainees and offers them legal advice, rejects the policy of prolonged detention.

More than 50 percent of detainees are eventually granted protection, he points out,

WHICH MEANS TRULY THEY ARE ASYLUM SEEKERS.

THEY ARE REFUGEES FOR ALL INTENTS AND PURPOSES...

[YET] PEOPLE BEING CONFINED IN DETENTION ARE GENERALLY PERCEIVED TO BE CRIMINALS.

J. SACCO 12-09

Whether or not they finally are deemed worthy of protection, the immigrants are locked up for months, kept under guard, surrounded by barbed wire, handcuffed when taken to hospital...

If irregular immigrants are treated like prisoners, is it any wonder that the Maltese assume they've done something wrong?

OPEN CENTERS

I wander into Tent No. 33 at the Hal Far Tent Village and introduce myself.

A couple of guys from Togo are sharing a pan of rice,

and a Somali named Abdullah is cooking some potatoes.

These men are so-called "freedoms," those immigrants finally released from detention to open centers, the last supervised stop before Malta tells them to fend for themselves.

Abdullah has lived here for a year, and he is "not satisfied" with his accommodations.

He says he's from a city, Mogadishu, and until he was assigned here, he'd only ever seen tents on television.

BEFORE I RAN FROM THE FIGHTING, BUT NOW I WANT TO RUN FROM THE TENTS...

J. SACCO 12-09

Since most all the men cannot find work, the monthly 130 Euros are crucial. The immigrants must buy their own food and everything else they need.

Abdullah's parents send him money from Somalia for clothes.

He leads me to a friend named Omar. Omar's time in detention and the tents has made him crazy, Abdullah claims.

I'm told Omar is so mentally damaged that he hasn't been signing for his 130-Euro allowance.

Haven't you alerted the staff, Abdullah?

I DID BUT THEY SAY, 'IT'S NOT OUR PROBLEM.'

He asks if there's anything I can do for Omar, and I agree to mention him at the office here myself.

Hoo boy! Looks like I've kicked a hornet's nest!

I didn't know I carried such weight!

Government employees are running into each other to check up on Omar's case!

Others do only too well.

I KNOW PEOPLE AT MARSA OPEN CENTER WHO CAN GIVE YOU 10,000 EUROS CASH, IF YOU NEED IT.

The open center was turned into a "mafia town," he says.

When small shops and kitchens were opened on site to "empower" the residents, a class of operators began treating the businesses as their own property, even selling "ownership" for thousands of Euros.

Meanwhile, the poorest immigrants are forced to buy from these shops and restaurants on credit.

BEFORE A PERSON RECEIVES HIS CHECK, HE'S ALREADY SPENT IT.

Bugri says he is battling to wrest control of the businesses from their "owners"— many of whom live off site — and is creating a cooperative that will let everyone benefit.

J. SACCO 12-09

There are ethnic tensions at the open center as well.

"All the shops were owned by Somalis," he says. "All the best rooms were Somali... And so they pushed the West Africans and Ethiopians to the back [rooms].

"There are fights, but the Somalis are the majority so they always win the fight."

Malta's policy has essentially created wide cracks for "freedoms" to fall through. Technically, the maximum period the immigrants are allowed to stay at the open centers is one year.

After that their monthly allowance is stopped and they are expected to move out and make it on their own.

Minister Mifsud Bonnici doesn't seem moved by my bleeding-heart concern for their future.

THEY JUST PARK THEMSELVES IN THOSE [CENTERS], AND THEY STAY THERE EXPECTING THE GOVERNMENT TO DO SOMETHING FOR THEM.

THEY HAVE TO FIGHT TO LIVE IN THE WESTERN WORLD...

IF YOU DO NOT PUSH THEM TO DO THIS, THEY DO NOT MOVE.

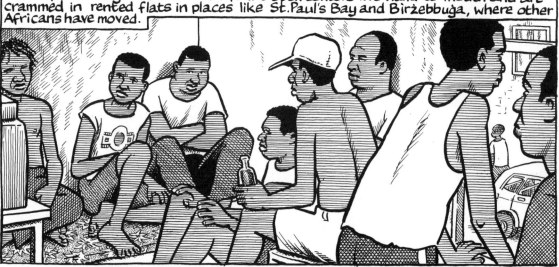

Most of the immigrants who have left the open centers live hand-to-mouth and are crammed in rented flats in places like St. Paul's Bay and Birżebbuġa, where other Africans have moved.

This, then, is what a "freedom" waiting out his year at an open center has to look forward to in a country that can barely stand the sight of him.

J. SACCO 12·09

147

Both men have been designated "rejects," meaning their asylum applications have been turned down.

Unlike immigrants granted humanitarian status, they can only get a work permit if a potential employer agrees to jump through bureaucratic hoops to sponsor them.

In other words: fat chance!

Their only hope is off-the-books day labor.

THEY ABANDON US HERE.

But surely the government has given you part of your monthly allowance as a start.

THEY GAVE US 24 EUROS TO BUY OUR CLOTHES, OUR FOOD, EVERYTHING.

Couldn't you take advantage of the free job training or educational benefits Malta claims to provide?

WE DON'T HAVE POTS. WE DON'T HAVE GAS. THAT 24 EUROS CANNOT BUY POTS AND PLATES.

WE USE THE MONEY TO EAT IN RESTAURANTS.

IF I START SCHOOL NOW... WHO WILL PAY TO FEED ME?

OUR TALENTS WILL DIE WITH US HERE.

But suddenly a van stops, and the guy from Togo doesn't wait to hear out Mohammed's lament.

Only one other fellow seems to have seen the vehicle.

There's a quick discussion with the driver, and then both men hop in.

Our Togolese pal has landed his first job.

YOU CAN'T INTE-GRATE THEM... WE'RE TOO DIFFER-ENT.

IN ENG-LAND THEY DON'T WANT THEM TO PUT A CROSS IN THE SCHOOL*...IF THEY DON'T WANT TO SEE THE CROSS, THEY SHOULD STAY IN SO-MALIA

THIS COUNTRY IS OURS, NOT THEIRS.

*ADDITIONALLY, IN NOV. 2009, A EUROPEAN COURT TOLD ITALY TO REMOVE CRUCIFIXES FROM THE WALLS OF STATE SCHOOLS.

ROMINA

I DON'T SEE ANY PROSPECT OF SETTLING DOWN [IN MALTA].

I WANT TO GO TO A COUNTRY WHERE I FEEL I BELONG...OR BACK TO ERI-TREA, IF PEACE COMES TO MY COUNTRY.

IT'S TRUE I'M LIVING IN MALTA, BUT IN REALITY I'M LIVING IN THE AFRICAN COM-MUNITY IN MALTA.

JOHN

INTEGRATION

Ahmed Bugri, the manager of the Marsa Open Center, married in Mal-ta and has lived here for almost two decades.

FOR THREE YEARS MY FATHER-IN-LAW TOLD ME HE DIDN'T WANT A BLACK MAN IN HIS FAM-ILY.

BUT NOW HE'S SEEN ME TAKE CARE OF MY WIFE...AND TAKE CARE OF MY CHILDREN.

NOW HE LOVES ME AS A SON.

One gets the impression the minister would drive them there himself, if only someone would take them, if only the Africans would —in a phrase he repeats over and over— **MOVE ON.**

But Mifsud Bonnici is a big-picture man.

He knows the Maltese voters, he knows the budgetary constraints, he needs to ease the pressure on a tiny nation straining under sudden social, cultural, and racial problems generated by wars, poverty, and climate change somewhere far, far away.

Francis Debono, the mayor of Marsa, knows the voters, too.

He and they live cheek-by-jowl with hundreds of African men at the open center.

He is much less hopeful than the minister that mainland Europe will integrate great numbers of Malta's Africans.

SOME OF THEM ARE GOING TO BE HERE FOR YEARS...

IN THE END, THE FEAR [OF] AND PITY FOR THEM ENDS.

BECAUSE YOU GET USED TO THEM, AND YOU HAVE TO LIVE IN THE REALITY THAT EXISTS.

WE ARE NOT TRYING TO INTEGRATE OURSELVES; WE ARE NOT TRYING TO LOOK AT THE FUTURE PROBLEMS.

YOU HAVE TO GIVE THEM SCHOOLS, MOSQUES, HEALTH TREATMENT... EVERYTHING THEY NEED, ACTUALLY.

J. SACCO 1-10

He worries about large concentrations of Africans dominating neighborhoods.

He worries that eventually the chronically underemployed "double rejects" will create criminal organizations.

In fact, he has almost every worry that every Maltese person has about their uninvited guests.

But Debono worries more that Malta is losing its way.

IF YOU HAVE A CHANCE TO HELP PEOPLE GET ON THEIR FEET, THEN YOU MUST.

YOU'RE TALKING ABOUT PEOPLE, NOT GRASS.

The Maltese, who play host to hundreds of thousands of European tourists every year, have long taken pride in their reputation for hospitality.

According to the 'Acts' of the apostles, St. Paul was shipwrecked here and struggled through the raging surf onto the island where the natives showed him and the other survivors "unusual kindness."

I reminded one of my relatives of this story and compared the reception of the Africans to that of St. Paul.

She would have none of it.

"But St. Paul was here for a while and left," she said.

I thought there was no better place to report on the issue of African migration to Europe than my own birthplace, Malta. For one thing, as a Maltese I figured local people would be less reticent with me about their feelings toward the Africans who had landed on the island. For another, though English is widely spoken there, it is not spoken by everyone, and my fair knowledge of the Maltese language would allow me to operate without a translator. Also, Malta is a small country, one of those places where one can make an appointment with the ministers and officials who are the chief architects and administrators of policy. Finally, this story could be easily told from the perspective of the Africans, who were approachable in the camps and centers where they lived and in the streets while they looked for work. Fortunately, with forty-eight pages, the *Virginia Quarterly Review* gave me plenty of room to cover all these bases. Though obviously my sympathies are with the migrants, who had endured tremendous hardships to reach such an unwelcoming place whatever their reasons for setting out across the Mediterranean Sea, I thought it was incumbent on me to treat the fears and apprehensions of the Maltese people seriously. Few peoples, I'm afraid, are up to the challenge of absorbing large and sudden influxes of outsiders, especially those of a different color. My own people are no better than anyone else.

"The Unwanted" appeared in the *Virginia Quarterly Review* in two parts in the Winter 2010 and Spring 2010 issues.

INDIA

Green Shirt was born into the Other Backward Classes, an officially designated group of castes who are generally disadvantaged but who consider themselves the human superiors of the Dalits.

Further up the scale are the Forward Castes —Brahmins, Rajputs, and others—before whom Dalits and Backward Classes obligingly bow and scrape.

In rural India especially, the caste-based tiers form daunting barriers to any sort of social or economic mobility and are the ready-made framework around which the vines of inequality twirl and thrive.

As if by right then, Green Shirt can hinder our meeting with the Musahars, he can barge in and try to stop it,

and if Brijesh manages to deflect him,

he can't contain a group of higher caste teenagers who suddenly surround the hut and peer over the Dalit women listening in.

161

We emerge, and as the boys close around us,

our host, Sib Charan, steps forward to address me.

LOOK, IT IS VERY GOOD THAT YOU ARE COMING HERE, BUT SINCE WE ARE NOT GOING ANYWHERE BECAUSE OF YOU—

he means to find work or food

—IT'S A PROBLEM.

TOMORROW WE WILL NOT MEET.

I'm taken aback. I hadn't considered how our daily visits might be interfering with the grim business of survival here in the Kushinagar district of Uttar Pradesh, one of India's poorest states.

"Big people." That's a euphemism for those who call the shots in the village, those who perhaps aren't so much worried that we'll glimpse the shameful poverty here as get an inkling into what a wonderful business it can be.

But now he gestures as if indicating the boys among us.

YOU KNOW THE PROBLEM.

BIG PEOPLE WILL GET ANNOYED.

J. SACCO 4.10

The boys escort us back to our car.

They are victorious.

They have chased the prying outsiders from their village.

DALIT PRIDE

Underneath the India of billion-aires and Bolly-wood stars, the India whose growth rate rivals China's, is a country in which more than three-quarters of the population — 836 million people — live on less than half a dollar a day and where the prevalence of underweight children is nearly double that of Sub-Saharan Africa.

The rural depths of Kushinagar represent the India that neither shines nor sparkles nor even flickers, where most people have next to noth-ing or nothing and where it is possible, through in-debtedness, to have even less.

KUSHINAGAR DISTRICT

DELHI

UTTAR PRADESH

KOLKATA

MUMBAI

INDIA

UTTAR PRADESH

LUCKNOW

GORAKHPUR

For the Musahars of the Gurumiha Mafitola hamlet, the Below the Poverty Line definition, which government committees endlessly recalibrate, is a moot point because the issue is not merely poverty, which might be bearable, but hunger.

That is their only concern: food.

The people here don't know how old they are, and few can tell you how their children died—

all the women we ask seem to have lost two or three.

THEY WERE FIVE OR SIX YEARS OLD WHEN THEY DIED. THEY WERE ILL.

THERE WAS NO MEDICINE.

LALI DEVI

There is no religion here and no politics.

ONCE IT'S DECIDED BY THE VILLAGE CHIEF THE ENTIRE VILLAGE AGREES TO IT, AND THAT'S HOW WE VOTE.

WE DON'T KNOW WHAT PARTY IT IS.

They cannot tell us the names of India's prime minister or Uttar Pradesh's chief minister, who is known simply as Mayawati.

Mayawati is a Dalit herself and the self-styled champion of her downtrodden kind.

J. SACCO 4·10

164

In the state capital, Lucknow, on a scale and at an expense that would make a Pharaoh blush, she has cleared enormous tracts of land on which she has built monuments to Dalit worthies and erected oversized statues of herself.

THE BHIMRAO AMBEDKAR MEMORIAL (WHICH INCLUDES 60 MARBLE ELEPHANTS)

In her fiery speeches she trumpets "Dalit Pride," but here in Kushinagar, the Dalits who bring out chairs for us at our first meeting will not dare to sit with upper caste visitors or a white man.

I mistake the building behind us for one of their homes, but they tell me it's a government school built five years ago.

But the teacher stopped teaching, they say, and he only showed up to shoot the breeze with the men — presumably while still drawing his paycheck.

He stopped coming around all together three months ago, they tell us.

Here they don't see any point in informing the authorities, and they won't send their kids to other schools nearby.

CHILDREN OF THE [HIGHER] CASTES START BEATING THEM...

IT WAS HERE THAT THEY WERE SAFE.

IF THEY OPEN IT AGAIN, [THE CHILDREN] WILL GO.

But Sib Charan's own son tells me he's never been to school before, apparently not even when classes were held here.

Indeed, what good would a little education do? Would it lead anywhere?

What does Sib Charan expect from his kids?

WE ASK THEM TO DO SOMETHING [TO] BRING SOME FOOD.

What does his wife, Suvanti, hope for their children?

I DON'T THINK ANYTHING ABOUT IT.

What does their son, Rajinder, want out of life?

I HAVE NO PLAN.

Here there is no electricity, no toilet, no 21st or 20th or 19th century convenience of any kind.

What the hamlet does have are three hand-operated water pumps, put in about ten years ago, and brick houses.

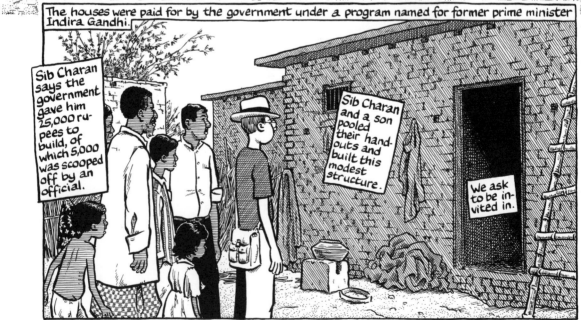

The houses were paid for by the government under a program named for former prime minister Indira Gandhi.

Sib Charan says the government gave him 25,000 rupees to build, of which 5,000 was scooped off by an official.

Sib Charan and a son pooled their hand-outs and built this modest structure.

We ask to be invited in.

J. SACCO 4·10

166

167

Here in Kushinagar women can be hired for much less than men, usually 30 rupees per day.

Suvanti says she works for 20. Does she know that the minimum wage is 100 rupees?

WHAT IS THE POINT OF KNOWING IT?

MEN MAKE 100 RUPEES, WOMEN MAKE 20 RUPEES.

HOW DOES IT MAKE A DIFFERENCE IF I KNOW?

In any case, agricultural jobs are steady only during the planting and harvesting season, which she says adds up to just two months a year.

It is March, and the last time there was any such work for most all the Dalits we talk to was in October or November when they brought in the rice crop.

Meanwhile, mechanization is slowly but surely making their labor superfluous.

BEFORE, WE USED TO GET SOME WORK. WE DON'T GET IT NOW...

MOST OF THE WORK IS DONE BY TRACTORS AND MACHINES.

ANGANI DEVI

To supplement their pitiful income, a government scheme supposedly provides jobs to the rural poor.

But none of the Dalits we meet worked more than a fraction of the 100 days guaranteed every year, and many had never even heard of the program.

J. SACCO 5-10

In fact, we find a general skepticism about education.

In some cases a child's labor value trumps whatever are the perceived benefits of sitting in class.

Some of the Musahars we meet in the village of Mainpur are lucky enough to find employment at a local brick kiln.

Mahant Prasad says,

OUR ENTIRE FAMILY GOES THERE ...EXCEPT MY MOTHER...

MY YOUNGEST DAUGHTER IS SEVEN YEARS OLD. SHE GOES ALSO.

At the kilns work is paid by the piece so if the tiniest hands can carry just a single brick at a time, they still would contribute something.

In the same village, we find that some of the Musahars inherited small fields doled out during previous government land redistribution schemes.

But most of them sold their land to buy the necessities their wages cannot cover and to pay off the loans they inevitably must take from money-lending sharks — who charge interest as high as 10 percent per month.

Jaishri Prasad, who has tuberculosis, sold his tiny plot to pay off a 30,000-rupee debt for medicine and food.

PROBLEM AFTER PROBLEM.

HIS WIFE, PHULA DEVI

Mahant Prasad sold his sixth of an acre to pay back a bank loan he took out to cover the grain he'd bought on credit.

ONE OF THE FOOD-GRAIN SHOP OWNERS TOOK MY LAND AND HE PAID [OFF] THE 25,000 RUPEES [I OWED] THE BANK AND THE OTHER SHOP-KEEPERS.

J. SACCO 5-10

Rajdeo sold part of his land to pay off a 10,000-rupee debt.

Can't he eke out some food from the remaining eighth of an acre?

THERE'S NO MONEY ...FOR SEEDS AND FERTILIZER AND ALL THAT.

In Sohrauvana village a mixed group of Dalits from the Chumar sub-caste and their equally poor Muslim neighbors gather in a cow shed to field our questions.

We have been talking for some time when I notice a young woman working her way forward.

Suddenly she is in front of us, demanding to know what all of the commotion is about.

If we are giving out benefits, she wants her name on the list.

I tell her we have come to find out about life here, that we have no benefits to give.

Her name is Astabul Nisha, and she says her husband is "extremely ill."

[THE AUTHORITIES] DON'T GIVE ANYTHING TO US.

WE EAT WHEN WE GET SOME WORK.

WE ARE DEPRIVED OF PRACTICALLY EVERYTHING.

NEITHER GOD NOR MEN, NO ONE IS THERE TO LISTEN TO US.

Later, in a hotel room in Gorakhpur, we meet a different sort of person, Ashok Choudhary, who was a leading local Dalit activist before turning to journalism.

He is a tired man who seems to sink into himself as he gives us his take on the plenitude of programs designed for the economic uplift of the downtrodden.

OUR FORMER PRIME MINISTER RAJIV GANDHI ADMITTED THAT 85 PERCENT OF MONEY SENT FOR DEVELOPMENT IS BEING SIPHONED OFF.

A SCHEME MEANS CORRUPTION...

THESE SCHEMES ARE MADE FOR MIDDLEMEN... NOT FOR THE POOR.

[THEY ARE] DESIGNED TO HELP THE CORRUPT IN MAKING MORE MONEY.

In fact, we find instances of the poor being asked to become poorer in order to access their benefits.

Bagmani from Kusumaha village says she has been told by her village chief to hand over 5,000 rupees if she wants to get on the list for a brick house.

SO FAR WE HAVEN'T GIVEN THE BRIBE.

Fatma from Sohrauvana village says she has been eligible for an old-age pension for two years but hasn't drawn a single payment because she hasn't paid a 5,000-rupee bribe.

HER UNSTAMPED PENSION BOOK

Her son was arrested for complaining about this at a village committee meeting.

I WAS A LITTLE LOUD AT THE TIME, AND THAT THEY DIDN'T LIKE.

J. SACCO 6-10

This is Upendra, the eldest of six brothers who have reclaimed the run-down, 150-year-old royal residence after the family lived elsewhere for decades. They intend to restore the building to its former luster.

AND IT WILL HAP-PEN...

THIS IS OUR IDENTITY. THIS IS OUR ROOT.

The family ruled for 1,000 years, he tells us.

It was a minor dynasty, but in its most glorious period, under the rule of Dilip Narayan Singh, who built the palace and for whom the area was renamed, its territory extended into the neighboring state of Bihar.

Would you rule again, I ask, if you had the chance?

YOU ARE TALKING THE IMPOSSIBLE.

Still, Upendra is happy to rhapsodize about his family's beneficent rule in that officially vanished feudal era.

THE OLDER PEOPLE WHO REMEMBER BEFORE INDEPENDENCE BELIEVE THAT PERIOD WAS BETTER.

THERE WAS DISCIPLINE, THERE WAS HONESTY, THERE WAS CHARACTER.

J. SACCO 6-10

"Earlier, every problem, including that of murder, used to be solved at this door," he says. "We used to [mete out] justice amicably. Now even a minor issue reaches the police."

But Upendra must still be held in some regal regard because Dalit and Other Backward Class villagers come seeking his mediation in family disputes and they respect his verdict, he says.

Have there been any improvements since the passing of the princely states?

Well, yes.

THOSE PEOPLE YOU ARE STUDYING, THE MUSAHARS, THEY HAVE CLOTHES TODAY, BUT JUST TEN YEARS AGO THEY WORE LOINCLOTHS... THEY HAD MUD HOUSES.

NOW EVEN THEIR CHILDREN ARE GOING TO SCHOOL.

I do not interrupt Upendra with the news that the Musahar children living nearby are searching for rat food instead of attending class.

J. SACCO 6.10

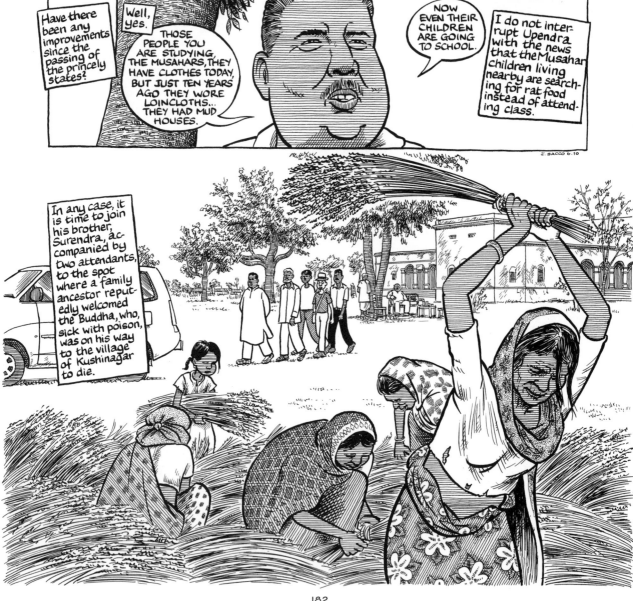

In any case, it is time to join his brother, Surendra, accompanied by two attendants, to the spot where a family ancestor reputedly welcomed the Buddha, who, sick with poison, was on his way to the village of Kushinagar to die.

182

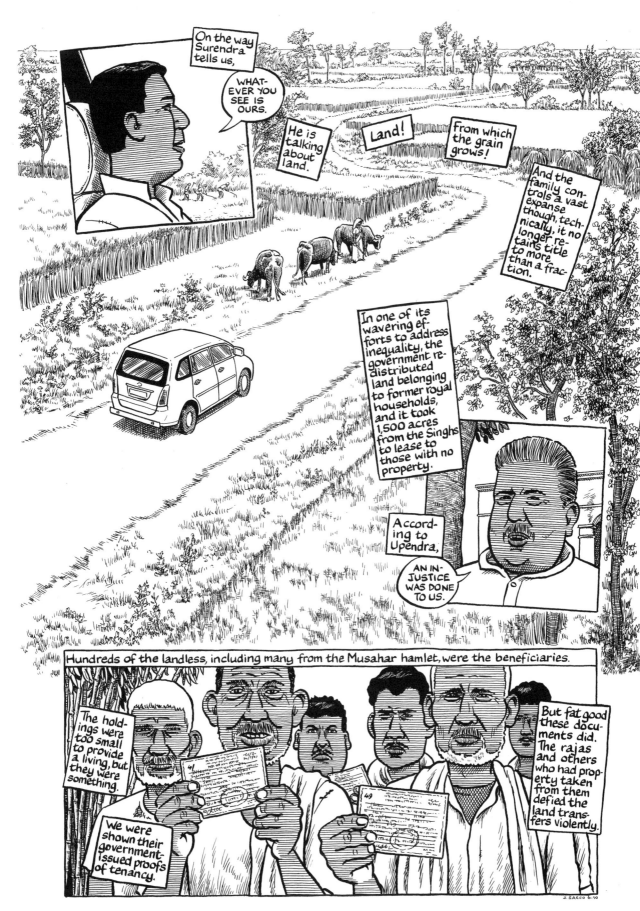

On the way Surendra tells us,

WHATEVER YOU SEE IS OURS.

He is talking about land.

Land!

From which the grain grows!

And the family controls a vast expanse though, technically, it no longer retains title to more than a fraction.

In one of its wavering efforts to address inequality, the government redistributed land belonging to former royal households, and it took 1,500 acres from the Singhs to lease to those with no property.

According to Upendra,

AN INJUSTICE WAS DONE TO US.

Hundreds of the landless, including many from the Musahar hamlet, were the beneficiaries.

The holdings were too small to provide a living, but they were something.

We were shown their government-issued proofs of tenancy.

But fat good these documents did. The rajas and others who had property taken from them defied the land transfers violently.

J. SACCO 6-10

184

Meanwhile, we've arrived at one of three Hindu temples that Surendra wants to show us.

This one is to the goddess Durga.

कुलकुला देदी

The lower forms watch us intently.

They give me the creeps.

One of them runs up and snatches something from a vendor in front of the shrine.

On the way to the next temple, dedicated to the god Shiva, I notice a particularly scruffy Dalit peeling himself off from the other gawkers to follow us.

Frankly, I don't like leaving my shoes at the entrance of each site — not with him standing around, anyway.

J. SACCO 6-10

By the time we get to the shrine of the god Bhairav, I'm certain he's going to snatch my shoes.

After a short ceremony at the tree, we head back to our shoes.

But now he's following us over a wide, dusty area, and he seems more focused on Surendra than on me.

The young attendant positions himself behind Surendra,

who, with practiced ease,

raises one foot,

and then the other,

while the Dalit maneuvers the shoes for the raja to step into.

And now it's time to see where Surendra's ancestors welcomed the Buddha.

THEY WILL BREAK OUR LEG

Did I tell you what we were whispering in that cooking hut that last day in Gurumiha Mafitola hamlet?

I had asked whether the Musahars there had the same charitable view of the rajas as the rajas had of themselves.

For example, would they think of going to any of the rajas for help or advice?

Sib Charan fixed me with his jaundiced eyes.

IF WE GO THERE, HE'LL KILL US. HE'LL BEAT US TO DEATH.

OUR GOAT HAD GONE THERE AND HE KILLED IT.

THEY WILL BREAK OUR LEG.

As for working for the rajas,

THEY WILL NOT PAY US PROPERLY.

OH MY GOD, OH MY GOD, HE HAS THOUSANDS OF ACRES OF LAND, BUT STILL HE DOESN'T PAY.

AND IF WE ASK ANYTHING, THEY WILL KILL US.

THEY HAVE A BIG MANGO ORCHARD, BUT IF I PICK UP A SINGLE MANGO IT WILL BE FATAL FOR ME.

As we pull away, I wonder how Dalits like these—

whose labor is all but superfluous,

whose only role seems to be attracting benefits that are easily plundered—

—can bust out of their dire circumstances.

I pose the question to Choudhary.

[WHEN] I WAS A POLITICAL ACTIVIST I USED TO TELL THEM TO EXERCISE THEIR POLITICAL RIGHTS AND ASSERT THEMSELVES, BUT NOW I DON'T SAY ANYTHING BECAUSE I KNOW WHENEVER THEY START RESISTING, THEIR SITUATION WILL FURTHER WORSEN.

THEY WILL BE ASSAULTED PHYSICALLY; THE POLICE WILL ARREST THEM...

WE CAN'T EXPECT THESE MOST POOR PEOPLE TO WAKE UP AND FIGHT AGAINST SUCH ODDS.

But what will become of Sib Charan, his wife Suvanti, Bhelu, and the other Musahars we have met?

Choudhary tells me that Musahars, known for their association with rats, are "extreme Dalits," hated by other Dalits, who "practice untouchability with them."

I BELIEVE THEY ARE A VANISHING RACE... BECAUSE IN 62 YEARS OF INDEPENDENCE, THEIR SITUATION HAS GONE FROM BAD TO WORSE

WHAT WILL HAPPEN IN ANOTHER 62 YEARS?

IT APPEARS OBVIOUS THAT ALL OF THEM WILL BE DEAD AND THEY WILL BE PART OF HISTORY.

India, Notes

The extraordinarily successful French magazine *XXI*, which specializes in long-form narrative journalism and doesn't take advertisements, is the publishing industry's greatest champion of comics reportage. It has regularly sent cartoonists out into the world and given them a good deal of magazine space—thirty pages each. Editor Patrick de Saint-Exupery, a seasoned journalist himself, was open to any idea I had and supportive at every step of the way. Once I decided to draw a comic about poverty in India, the problem I had was narrowing my focus. I could have examined the notorious farmer suicides or the urban slums, but I wanted to get off the beaten track. The author Pankaj Mishra passed me along to Indian journalist Piyush Srivastava, who suggested I visit Kushinagar and who graciously agreed to be my guide. We met in Lucknow, where he is based, and drove for a day to reach the district, where many of the dalits—people regarded by many Indians as "untouchables"—

are experiencing not just abject poverty but real hunger. My idea was to go to one village and get to know its inhabitants well over the course of a week or so. As detailed in the story, after three visits to the same hamlet, Piyush and I were essentially chased out of the area by higher caste individuals who did not like us snooping around. We decided to visit other villages, but briefly, for no more than a couple of hours each, to avoid the same result. I would have preferred not to do such hit-and-run journalism, but it was unavoidable under the circumstances and had the benefit of giving us a broader survey of conditions in the area.

"Kushinagar" appeared originally in French in *XXI*, no. 13, January/February/March 2011.

ACKNOWLEDGMENTS

This book encompasses stories from many trips to several countries over more than ten years and a full list of all those who have helped me along the way would go on for pages. Numerous journalists, fixers, translators, and others have schooled me, showed me how to be careful, and provided me with company and friendship. To them I am forever grateful.

But this time allow me to shift the focus away from colleagues in "the field" to acknowledge a few individuals who made a difference years before I got my first press pass. I am referring to certain teachers at Sunset High School in Portland, Oregon. (I had a few good professors in college too, but for me, as a whole experience, high school was more dense and intimate.)

I took my first journalism class from Brenda Holman. After she moved on, Sandra Ku took over. Both were superb instructors. I owe them a great debt for their encouragement and for instilling in me a love for rigorous news writing. They showed me that journalism was mostly fun and, when not quite fun, personally rewarding, which is how it has felt to me ever since, even under trying circumstances and even when the subject matter has been distasteful. Most important, they made me feel that good reporting mattered.

Hal Swafford was my history teacher. I didn't need to be convinced that history was interesting, but Mr. Swafford (I call him Hal now, but Mr. Swafford in this context sounds more appropriate) emphasized understanding the relationship between events rather than being able to recite them in the correct chronological order. "Think!" he used to command, tapping the side of his head, and he showed his students how. This book is dedicated to him and to Paul Copley, another esteemed teacher at Sunset High School, whose classes I never took but who entered my life decades later. Together with Hal and two Sunset grads, Rich LaSasso and Mike Stevens, I would meet Paul for drinks every few weeks at Cassidy's in downtown Portland. Those meetings brought out the best in us, I think, and in me certainly. There is no bullshitting ex–high school teachers like Hal and Paul, no saying a bunch of nonsense without being able to back it up with facts, and their opinion of me and my thoughts still matters terribly. Paul's passing was a real blow.

I also wish to thank my parents. I think they had misgivings about my studying journalism and even more misgivings when I seemed to give up journalism to draw comics. But they're proud of me now and see the value in what I do, and doesn't parental approval count as a victory in this world? Finally, I want to thank Amalie, who has put up with my long absences and never questioned my need to go places to see things. Leaving home with her heartfelt support has meant a great deal.

ABOUT THE AUTHOR

JOE SACCO, one of the world's greatest cartoonists, is widely hailed as the creator of war reportage comics. He is the author of, among other books, *Palestine*, which received the American Book Award, and *Safe Area Goražde*, which received the Eisner Award for best graphic novel and was named a *New York Times* Notable Book and *Time* magazine's best comic book of 2000. His most recent book, *Footnotes in Gaza*, was the first graphic novel to win the Ridenhour Book Prize, was short-listed for a *Los Angeles Times* Book Award, and also received an Eisner Award. Sacco's work has been translated into fourteen languages and his comics reporting has appeared in *Details*, *The New York Times Magazine*, *Time*, *Harper's*, and *The Guardian*, among other publications. He lives in Portland, Oregon.